The ITT Key Issues Lecture Series

is made possible through a grant from
International Telephone and Telegraph Corporation

This series of lectures took place in the latter months of 1976
and the spring of 1977 at the University of Texas at Dallas.

International Business Prospects 1977-1999

Edited by
Howard F. Van Zandt
University of Texas at Dallas

With a foreword by
Harold S. Geneen

Bobbs-Merrill Educational Publishing
Indianapolis

The Bobbs-Merrill Company, Inc.

4300 West 62nd Street

Indianapolis, Indiana 46268

First Edition
First Printing 1978

International business prospects, 1977-1999.

(The Key issues lecture series)

Series of 7 lectures given in 1976-1977 at the University of Texas at Dallas.

CONTENTS: Van Zandt, H. F. Introduction: the problem areas.—Hall, E. T. Prospects for improving human relations overseas.—Lindsay, Sir J. An overview of Europe, the Middle East, and Africa.—Rojko, A. S. The choices before us. [etc.]

1. International business enterprises—Addresses, essays, lectures. 2. Commerce—Addresses, essays, lectures. 3. Economic history—1945-   —Addresses, essays, lectures. I. Van Zandt, Howard F.

HD 2755.5.I537   330.9'04   78-15745

ISBN 0-672-97221-2

ISBN 0-672-97220-4 pbk.

Contents

Preface

Raymond P. Lutz

Dean, School of Management and Administration
University of Texas at Dallas

This book, *International Business Prospects 1977-1999,* will, we hope, help meet the needs of those who are wondering what is going to happen in this field in the remaining years of this century. No one knows, of course, precisely what is going to take place even a week in advance, much less in twenty-three years, but the authors are experts in their fields, and their views are deserving of careful consideration.

The century thus far has been one of the most exciting in the history of mankind. It started in the horse and buggy era and is now in the space age. It is hoped that with the great advances made in science mankind will, somehow or other, be able to solve his problems far better than has been done in the past.

We wish to express our appreciation to the International Telephone and Telegraph Corporation for the grant that enabled us to bring the Key Issues Lectures to the University. We also wish to thank Professor Howard F. Van Zandt who organized the series here and edited this volume.

Foreword

Harold S. Geneen

Chairman of the Board
International Telephone and Telegraph Corporation

St. Augustine is credited with considering time as a three-fold present: the present as we now experience it, the past as present in our memory, and, the future as a present expectation. The future, then, need not be some immeasurable leap toward a vague horizon; it actually begins in the here and the now.

The Key Issues Lecture Series at the University of Texas at Dallas affords one a rare opportunity today to become both a student and an investigator of the future. In this period of social change and economic uncertainty, it would appear to be a rather risky and ambitious task. The target is the year 1999, a year when most of today's graduates are likely to be at the midpoint of their professional careers.

The world on the eve of the twenty-first century will be, most likely, committed to existing programs. The framework of day-to-day life then should remain much the same as it is now. A complex society, such as ours, simply is not altered radically overnight. The manifold problems confronting us now are not likely to disappear to any great degree before the end of this century.

This does not discount the fact that there will be certain substantial changes. If we view the past as a present memory, we can see that our postindustrial domestic economy shifted from the product sector to the service sector.

The most subtle structural change is that technology itself is constantly undergoing modification. Technology should not be construed as building toward tomorrow's "better mousetrap." Rather, it is a highly disciplined, systematic, and efficient approach to meet desired objectives.

And, as industrial technology advances on the drawing boards and in the laboratories, it will marshal other disciplines in a cooperative effort to reach solutions faster and on a broader plane. The development of econometric models and computer forecasting are but two examples that come immediately to mind.

I believe further, that the wellsprings of future innovation will be found equally between our entrepreneurial private sector, if allowed to operate in a free economy, and within our intellectual institutions, primarily our universities and research organizations.

Fortunately, we need not wait until 1999 to glimpse the possibilities of the future since this excellent study projects the reader forward across the time-space bridge.

Any study of the future requires a multidisciplinary approach and this volume reflects a wide range of scholarly and professional thought. Dean Raymond P. Lutz and Professor Howard F. Van Zandt have organized a well-balanced series of overviews of international business prospects, problems, and opportunities.

I'm confident the perceptive observations herein will stimulate others to apply a similar methodology in comprehensive planning for the future. My congratulations to all on an excellent effort.

Introduction: The Problem Areas

Howard F. Van Zandt

Van Zandt, a native of Illinois, is currently Professor of International Management Studies at the University of Texas at Dallas. He lived in Japan for three periods totaling twenty-seven years, is a past President of the American Chamber of Commerce in Japan, and served on its Board of Governors for fifteen years. In June 1972, he was awarded the Order of the Rising Sun by the Emperor of Japan. Later that year he retired from his positions as ITT Senior Officer in Japan, Vice-President ITT Far East and Pacific, Inc., and Director and ITT Shareholders Representative in the Nippon Electric Co. and Sumitomo Electric Industries Co., returning to the U.S. to organize the International Management Studies program at the University.

A consultant on the technique of doing business in Japan, he has authored some 500 journal articles and several books on this and related subjects. He is a frequent speaker before conventions and clubs.

With international business growing at a far more rapid rate than domestic business, it is self-evident that nations are more dependent upon one another than ever before. This trend is accelerating, too.

In the not-too-distant past, university catalogues contained few if any courses in international business. Now this has changed, and institutions of higher learning are adding programs in international business as fast as they can recruit qualified instructors.

Additionally, private training firms have commenced offering a wide choice of seminars and courses in world business. Businessmen's associations have also entered the field and it is now possible to obtain practical guidance in major cities throughout the United States, Canada, Western Europe, and Japan.

Although universities and other training institutions cover most phases of world economic activity satisfactorily, there is one topic that is missing: forecasting the future. Many firms not only want guidance in the practicalities of everyday foreign management matters, but also want input that would enable them to prepare long-range plans.

Recognizing the importance of this, the International Management Studies Department of the University of Texas at Dallas, with a grant from the International Telephone and Telegraph Corporation, sponsored a series of seven public lectures beginning in December 1976 and continuing into the spring of 1977. The lectures, which took place at the University, attracted an audience of business executives, as well as graduate students, government officials, and faculty. The lectures were also broadcast through a closed circuit TV network to other universities in the area and to several major Dallas area firms.

These lectures have been combined into this book. It should be noted that in several instances the authors updated statistical data released subsequent to their presentations.

The speakers, as will be noted from the brief biographies, had personal expertise in the subjects covered. Each drawing from his own experience and studies attempted to forecast where we will be going from 1977 on through the end of the century.

The editor wishes to express his appreciation to Neil W. Hesse of Garland, Texas, for his assistance in editing these papers. Mr. Hesse, who has traveled widely abroad, is himself engaged in international business and was able to make many helpful suggestions.

The subject matter and positions taken by each contributor are discussed in the synopses following, together with the reflections of the editor.

HALL: PROSPECTS FOR IMPROVING HUMAN RELATIONS OVERSEAS

Anyone who has, over the years, watched businessmen from different countries as they negotiated would likely agree with Edward

'I'. Hall's statement, "Understanding human relations may well be the most important, exciting problem of this era." Blunders and miscalculations far too often complicate negotiations and at times bring disharmony and failure.

To see a skilled negotiator in action in a foreign environment, on the other hand, is a delight. He knows what to say, how to say it, and when. He also knows when NOT TO SAY anything. The Japanese and Koreans, for instance, are expert in using silence as a negotiating technique, and people from the European-Mediterranean culture are at a disadvantage when confronted by it.

Too often human beings assume that members of other cultures think exactly as they do and react as they do, too. While it is true that all healthy human beings will jump when pricked by a pin, in other situations, reactions will be different. The Japanese, for instance, like indirection, and their language is full of subtleties and ambiguities. Americans are noted worldwide for their directness and frankness. Japanese are self-demeaning (even though inwardly proud); to many foreigners, Americans seem boastful (probably made so by long exposure to advertising claims).

People who grow up in a culture that emphasizes numbers often forget that there are other influences that move people besides the ability to get something for, say, $5.98 instead of $6.03. A salesman dealing with natives of a country he has studied, whose history he knows and whose customs he respects, is more likely to make a sale than the salesman who has none of this background, but pitches his sale exclusively on price. A native of such a country explained it to me one time in this way: "If a foreigner goes to the trouble to study our culture and takes the time to understand us and like us, then I feel that I should be able to depend on him not to cheat me. I feel safer giving him an order than giving one to a man who knows only figures."

Professor Hall, as an anthropologist with long experience working with people of many different races, gives wise advice. If we human beings are to attain the successes we so sincerely desire in international relations, whether business or political, we had better try harder to learn how to improve human relations.

LINDSAY: AN OVERVIEW OF EUROPE, THE MIDDLE EAST, AND AFRICA

There is no area on earth that is likely to change more in the remaining years of the century than the Middle East and Africa.

International business investment naturally moves to countries where there is reasonable political and socioeconomic stability. The OPEC (Organization of Petroleum Exporting Countries) countries have stability and—realizing that the time is not too far away when their rich oil and gas deposits will be exhausted—are building industry as rapidly as plants can be imported and erected. The Republic of South Africa, which has by far the highest living standards on that continent, is quietly increasing its trade with newly independent black nations, to their mutual benefit. The Arab nations who don't have oil are to some extent benefiting from the largesse of those who do.

The situation in Europe is, as always, complicated. Sir James Lindsay describes the problems that must be solved if the EEC nations are to enjoy superpower status by the year 2000. Unless threatened from outside, one may wonder if the EEC members will ever abandon their historical independence, and group together in a political union.

The Soviet Union will apparently continue to grow steadily in economic strength. There are those who forecast that, as the Russians and their East European neighbors become rich, they will become less radical in their political beliefs.

Perhaps the Communists in the Eastern Bloc of countries will be influenced by the Communist parties in such Western states as Italy, France, and Spain. Dialogue between the two groups could lead to better relations between the capitalist and Communist nations as a whole. The Western Communists are learning, especially from their experience in Italy where they have won control of governments of many municipalities, that success in the polls brings responsibility too.

With this in mind, any talk in the United States of a return to isolationism or military withdrawal from Europe because of growth of Communist parties in the EEC, is, as Sir James states, a counsel of despair.

ROJKO: THE CHOICES BEFORE US—ALTERNATIVE WORLD FOOD BALANCES TO THE YEAR 2000

Mr. Rojko has suggested two choices for alternative world food balances, either of which could be adopted. In Alternative I, he postulates a modified continuation of the trends of the 1950s, 1960s, and early 1970s. In Alternative II, he shows what is likely to occur if there is a slowing in population growth, plus higher incomes, and better organization of agriculture in the less developed countries.

There is certainly room for improvement in food production techniques in many developing countries. As one expert pointed out, it is not easy to teach crop rotation and fertilizer uses to natives who are so primitive that they couldn't even tie their shoes—if they had any, which they don't.

The projections Mr. Rojko has made are reasonable and attainable based upon such knowledge as we possess at this time. We don't know, of course, if nitrogen fertilizer usage will have to be drastically curtailed, on the basis that it may be as harmful to the ozone layer as fluorocarbons from aerosol cans. We don't know if there will be climatic changes. We don't know how soon subsurface water reserves will be exhausted. We don't know where war will strike and how it might affect the transport of food to import-dependent workshop nations such as the United Kingdom and Japan. We don't know if agriculturally productive areas will be turned temporarily into deserts through defoliation or nuclear bombings. These are all unknowns, but it is equally possible that man through his technical genius may develop new ways of growing food, ways that will enable developing overpopulated countries to come closer to feeding themselves.

The United States, Canada, and other food-surplus nations have through their generosity given enormous quantities of food to developing nations. With populations rising virtually unchecked in many of the latter, the time is coming when the food-surplus countries will have only enough to meet either the demands of longtime buyers such as Japan and the United Kingdom, or else the demands of nonpaying countries who have not taken effective steps to reduce their birthrates as well as to increase their own food production. What will happen when there won't be enough for both?

It might be a good time for the developing nations to consider the measures listed in Alternative II of Mr. Rojko's paper.

Study of East Asia and Oceania reveals that some nations have cultures or "systems" that work well: the most conspicuous examples are Japan, Taiwan, Singapore, Hong Kong, Australia, and New Zealand with the Republic of Korea fast moving into the "successful" group. Each of these countries has a rate of literacy of over 75 percent with a practical maximum of 98 percent plus in Japan, Australia, and New Zealand; it should also be noted that the birth rates in these nations are comparatively low.

With the wars occurring in each decade from the 1930s to the 1970s now past, the nations of the area seem headed for a period of steady economic development. If war can be avoided, there is probably no other area whose growth in the next twenty-three years will be at as rapid a rate.

Japan, which led all industrial nations in the rate of economic growth from 1950 until 1975, is not expected to keep up this high rate, but still should do well. Due partly to better disciplined labor unions than in most other industrial countries, the productivity of Japanese factories continues to rise faster than elsewhere. Japan's success in export markets and the high prices of U.S. goods led to the devaluation of the dollar in late 1971 and again in 1973. Although other forces also contributed to the decline in the dollar in the 1977-78 devaluation, Japan's invasion of the U.S. market was of major weight. There are those who think that the twenty-first century will be Japan's century and see her as the most prosperous of industrial countries.

The most difficult problem to solve in the area is the ill will between the People's Republic of China and the Soviet Union. China with a population of possibly 950,000,000 is expected to grow to about 1,350,000,000 by the end of the century. The pressures on the Chinese to expand into sparsely settled, but mineral-rich Siberia and the Mongolian People's Republic will be strong for an indefinite period. The Chinese have already moved in such large numbers into the Inner Mongolian provinces that Chinese now outnumber Mongols there by ten to one.

Provided birth rates are reduced substantially, it is likely that Southeast Asia will thrive too. There are extensive mineral resources in the Philippines, Thailand, Malaysia, and Indonesia; in a world that is exhausting its mineral reserves the value of those hidden in the jungles of Southeast Asia will rise rapidly during the rest of the century.

Shaw's paper points out that at least one futurologist predicts that annual two-way trade between the United States and East Asia-Oceania might total nearly $710,000,000,000 by the year 2000. This is possible provided war doesn't rear its ugly head, the energy shortage is solved, and people in developing countries reduce their birth rates. Who knows!

VOSS: WORLD ENERGY NEEDS 1977-1999

As Voss points out, man has been pushed into using each new source of energy because the old had reached its limits. In the case of oil, however, the dependence of the world on it will come to an end primarily because the supply will be exhausted. In earlier times, our ancestors used firewood and windmills. While we may still use both, there is not enough firewood to meet our needs; the same is true of hydroelectric power and coal. Streams are still being dammed, and coal is still being mined although not enough is being produced.

Many other potential sources of power—sources which could be exploited as we run out of oil—could be developed, according to Voss. Will private industry be allowed to develop these sources—and profit while doing so—or will the heavy hand of government so complicate these businesses as to make them uneconomic?

Voss makes a good case for conservation, urging that each of us can and must conserve if we are to preserve our way of life until new sources of energy come in view. During the energy crunch that accompanied the oil boycott, Americans became conscious of the need to reduce heating, air conditioning, and unnecessary automobile driving. We could curtail our consumption of oil and natural gas again if the importance of doing so were brought home in the effective way it was during the boycott.

The shortage of natural gas in the northern states in the winter of 1976-77 is likely to be repeated, for we are depleting our sources. The realities will be brought home after one or two more severe winters.

There are those who feel that the energy shortage will lead to international political problems. Nations like Sweden and Japan, for instance, which must import virtually all their oil, hope that as Middle East oil runs out, their neighbors will share their own production. The Swedes may not think they should have to curtail their industry, while the Norwegians keep their own going full blast aided by North Sea wells. The Japanese may feel abused if they have to reduce factory output while their neighbors in China and Siberia have plenty of oil and natural gas.

When the energy crunch becomes severe, as Voss's figures indicate it will, possibly a United Nations commission will be organized to ration the little oil that is available. The political implications are enormous.

WOLF: INTERNATIONAL BUSINESS IN LATIN AMERICA: AN OVERVIEW OF THE YEAR 2000

Some optimistic predictions about the future of Latin America are outlined by William Wolf who bases them on reports of the Trilateral Commission, a group whose members come from Europe, North America, and Japan. However, he admits that there are many serious problems in the nations south of the U.S. border, including most importantly, the difference between the rich and the poor.

Although there are national rivalries, they have not led to devastating wars for about 100 years. Hopefully, the numerous territorial and other disputes that still exist and occasionally inflame public opinion will be settled peacefully. Even the revolutions, which are more numerous in Latin America than in the entire rest of the world, are not usually accompanied by much, if any, bloodshed.

We Americans have a special interest in our neighbors to the south, even though their cultures are far more different from ours than are those of any European nation. Even the Japanese find the culture of the U.S. to be a familiar one, by comparison with those of the Spanish and Portuguese-speaking nations.

Among the examples Wolf points out is the disparity in the standard of living between the people of Mexico and those of the U.S. With the unemployment rate in Mexico close to 40 percent, and little or no opportunity at home, it is inevitable that Mexicans will try to emigrate to the United States illegally. The 1900-mile border, unlike borders between most other countries, is, for the most part, unfenced. Although the U.S. wants to be a good neighbor, it is obvious that there is a limit to the number of Mexicans it can admit. If Mexico's birth rate continues at existing high levels, the population will rise from 65,000,000 to about 140,000,000 by the end of this century. Since Mexico has been unable to feed its population from its own production since it reached 52,000,000, it is possible that 75,000,000 Mexicans could want to emigrate in the next twenty-three years. Should the United States permit such a large invasion, American politico-social-economic stability would be threatened.

To avoid this disaster, the United States must give great attention to the border and to the nation south of it.

EDGELL: INTERNATIONAL TOURISM AND TRAVEL

As the world's supply of raw materials used in manufacture diminishes, it is obvious that the economic structure built largely on supplying the tangible needs of consumers must undergo a radical alteration. For example, people want things made of metals, wood, plastics, and paper, yet the capacity to make these is being eroded because basic raw materials are being depleted. What will happen to our economy when articles made of such materials are no longer obtainable cheaply and plentifully as in the past? Will we have a dreadful depression because of forced reduction in production?

As one may see from reading Edgell's paper, human needs are changing. Our demand for things we can feel and touch will decline and in the future there will be more interest in travel and tourism, an industry which is not built on a tangible product.

Travel-tourism permits its customers to enjoy what they wish merely by looking, listening, and enjoying fragrance and taste. It is mostly educational and, as such, is a step forward and upward in man's evolution.

Those who travel abroad may be expected to have greater perspective in their outlook and to be better informed on foreign matters. Hopefully, they will be more tolerant and understanding and far more appreciative of other cultures. Americans, Russians, and Chinese—

each notoriously poor in foreign languages—may study the tongues spoken in the countries they visit.

Americans are often puzzled by the interests of visitors from overseas. To a Texan, there is nothing noteworthy in the vast flat plains in the Panhandle. To a Japanese, however, the prospect of seeing a part of the world where there are no mountains and hills is thrilling, for in his homeland he is never out of sight of mountains.

Many Americans think of travel-tourism in terms of flights to such places as Ireland, Poland, Italy, or Israel. Most of the natives of those four countries, however, would far more like to see the United States than to explore their own homelands. One aspect about the travel-tourism business is that if properly conducted, it can meet the needs of all.

The United States, as Edgell explains, should do what it can to eliminate or reduce impediments to international tourism. Anyone anywhere who has the intellectual curiosity to travel, the financial means to pay his way, and a willingness to obey the laws of host countries should be encouraged.

ONE

Prospects for Improving

Human Relations Overseas

Edward T. Hall

Formerly Professor of Anthropology at Northwestern University, Edward Hall is best known for his books, The Silent Language, The Hidden Dimension, *and* Beyond Culture. *Hall's writings are concerned with creating better understanding of the human equation in intercultural relations and in man's use of space.*

Known for his early research in the conduct of foreign relations and intercultural communication, he was Director of the State Department's Point IV Training Program for five years. Later his special interest in space led to the development of proxemics, the study of man's use of space as a human activity.

He is a consultant to architects, business, government, and private foundations and currently lives in Santa Fe, New Mexico.

THE CHALLENGE OF HUMAN RELATIONS

Understanding human relations may well be the most important, exciting problem of this era. In my opinion, improving human relations is easily the most difficult task facing us today. To speak on this topic is both a privilege and a challenge—one which I approach with trepidation—having spent two-thirds of my life working in this field.

Quite frankly, whenever I think about the subject I become either frightened or depressed. Fortunately, these emotional states are only temporary because basically I am an optimist. To me the future looks much better than the past, provided Americans can give up some of their stereotypes about the other people of the world. Before developing this point, let me first describe a paradox of human relations.

Why is human relations such a thorny, complex subject when all you have to do is be nice to people and treat them the way you like to be treated? As an anthropologist, I favor George Bernard Shaw's golden rule: "Don't do unto others as you would have them do unto you. They might not like it." Shaw's maxim should be tatooed on everyone who works abroad, preferably in a prominent place of high visibility. The projecting of one's own culture onto other people is not unique to Americans, however, because most human beings spend their lives trying to "control their inputs" according to a system of internal reference signals about which they know little, if anything. This system of "reference signals" is internalized early in life, molded by culture. The wife and mother who keeps a neat, tidy house is only trying to satisfy a somewhat unforgiving, obsessional individual who lurks behind the closed doors of her psyche, but who jumps out like a jack-in-the-box the minute an ash hits the rug. The cultural program most of us have grown up with required thousands of years or more to reach its present state, and because it functions largely out of conscious awareness, it is hard to change.

Meshing Business Subcultures

In any discussion of the future of interpersonal relations in business overseas, there are always those who would say that it is only the "bottom line" that counts, and if your price is right you can always sell, so why bother with interpersonal relations? I was once told by the vice-president in charge of foreign operations for one of *Fortune's* 500 that he doubted very much if any significant amount of business was lost because the representatives of American firms "didn't have good manners." This was twenty-five years ago. Maybe he's whistling a different tune today, but I doubt it. Attitudes of this sort do not change easily, because each of us lives in his own world, playing the game by hidden rules.

Howard Van Zandt, who so ably represents the University of Texas at Dallas' International Management Studies Department, spent many years of his life in Japan. He knows that any American executive who operates on the assumption that manners don't count would not do well for his company in Japan today. I have known and worked with many businessmen in the U.S. who were successful and gifted in human relations; yet there were always others who didn't understand the relationship of worker or staff morale to productivity, a human relations problem if there ever was one. One must pose the question: how then are these people going to understand it abroad? My son, who once was in the hotel business, observed that dissatisfied employees can cause a hotel to go broke. Hotel management frequently is not even aware that they are violating the mores of key groups of employees. Yet, as this observation suggests even at home in the U.S., business is made up of subcultures. One of the jobs of management, is to get all these subcultures to mesh—not always an easy thing to do— and how much more difficult this must be abroad.

Some of the problems American business encounters overseas can be traced to the fact that all too frequently little importance is attached to these same problems at home. Then, there is that old familiar dichotomy between the job and human relations. Frequently executives feel they must put results ahead of human relations, and it is difficult to convince them they may be wrong because performance is measured by earnings per share. It is often said that in the U.S. it is the bottom line that counts, but looking ahead, I doubt very much that this will always be true. People all over the world are being forced by changing times to abandon oversimplified models of performance. This new world will require a different kind of manager—one who may be less hard-nosed but also less naive about the realities of business life, and less committed to reliance on cut-and-dried figures to the exclusion of all else. Managers are learning that organizations are first, last, and always made up of people. Before expanding on this particular point, it is necessary to stop and ask ourselves why people are so important.

Most of us are forever satisfying someone, even if it is a partially hidden taskmaster of our own making, who looks over our shoulder while we work, or the voice of a conscience that keeps us from overstepping bounds established by those people who helped mold our personality when we were growing up. Some of us have to satisfy relatively few people in the course of our daily life, others have a more difficult time and walk an imaginary tightrope because of the large number of people to be satisfied. One can only relate to these real and illusory people in one way: personally, or more specifically, interpersonally. Sometimes we relate through an intermediary or by means of our extensions, including such prestigious items as Cadillacs, Picassos, et cetera. But these status symbols are directed *to someone.* No matter how hard we try, there are always people who are being influenced by and who respond to what we do and have. Even a hermit by the very act of separating himself from society calls attention to his ideas. Buildings are a tangible example of what I am talking about. The architect has people to satisfy before he even puts pencil to paper. First, there are his own built-in critics who represent esthetic standards that he must meet, and then his client or clients. Further, there are other architects—perhaps those on AIA juries who make awards. These are followed by the public, the users of the building, as well as a rather ephemeral melange whom we'll call *posterity.* Yet, when we look at a building, few of us realize that behind the design lies a host of interpersonal encounters. It doesn't stop there either, because the occupants of the building are constantly reminded of whether or not the architect considered their needs when he designed the building. His efforts will either enhance or impede their work, depending on how well he did his job. A building then is truly a multilevel communication, and it is precisely this model that I would like to apply to the international scene.

A Multilevel Approach

I chose this model rather than the cultural model, because while the cultural model has proved to be workable for anthropologists, it simply does not translate easily to overseas business. It is paradoxical that when one talks about the subculture of machinists, plasterers, waitresses, bell boys, lawyers, doctors, or managers, there is little difficulty in understanding what is meant. Yet, when we refer to the culture of the Japanese, the Chinese, the French, or English it is often hard to convey what really differentiates them from us. To be able to describe in real-life terms how different cultures influence perception and structure the strategic building blocks of life is one of life's greatest challenges. However, if one considers the foreign scene from the viewpoint of human relations instead of some abstract notion called "culture," things take on a radically different look. By using a human relations model against a worldwide backdrop, it is soon apparent that we in the United States are underdeveloped in human relations skills. We are just beginning to learn what much of the rest of the world has known for a long time—that everything hinges on people and how one relates to them, as John F. Kennedy discovered during his first encounter with Khrushchev.

All peoples of the world must overcome built-in obstacles, but we in the United States appear to have a triple handicap: first, the practice of placing human relations at the bottom of the scale and "results" at the top, a false dichotomy if there ever was one. Second, an unstated view that foreigners and minorities are underdeveloped, and, third, a limited inventory of responses to those who are different. When someone looks down on others for whatever reason, he immediately limits his options at a time when it is important to increase them. I am reminded of a series of cross-cultural encounters described by a graduate student enrolled at Northwestern University's School of Management. Pierre was French and had worked for two American firms in his country. Managers of both firms couldn't understand why it took a French salesman so long to sell a new customer. Being French, Pierre knew that if he didn't know virtually *everything* about his customers, he couldn't relate to them. Building personal relationships was mandatory before even a word was said about business. Like most French salesmen, he took months to land a new account but once sold, the account could be counted on to be loyal for generations, which is why in many parts of Europe, the salesman—not the company—"owns" the customers. There is more to be discovered about Pierre, particularly his attitude toward selling.

What I'm about to describe is a system of obligations and incentives quite foreign to the American. Whenever Pierre was on the road and felt discouraged or blue or tired, he would think about all the people back at the office: Marie, who was supporting her mother and a small child; Philippe, who had medical bills to be paid because of his sick wife; Josephine, who was putting her brother through the university. He would say to himself, "All those people are depending on me and I must sell for them! If I don't sell, the company is in jeopardy and so are their jobs. I am selling for Marie's mother and child, Philippe's wife and Josephine's brother. I can't afford to sit here feeling sorry for myself." In the meantime, his manager from the States assumed that he had to lean on this man in order to "make plan."

Making Oneself Real Overseas

My point is not whether people around the world are the same or different underneath, but the fact that they are integral parts of networks made up of people to whom they are beholden. These individuals have loyalties and ways of expressing their loyalties—things they take for granted, attitudes towards friends and friendship and what friendship means that are quite distinct from what we are accustomed to at home. In one Southeast Asian country you simply do not exist (you are like a ghost) until you have established a firm relationship with specific individuals. Taking on substance as a known factor in a complex set of human equations is *not* accomplished overnight. It makes no difference how important you or your organization may be. You still have to make yourself real to them by making them real to yourself.

American attitudes toward money make us vulnerable because we seem to think that money can solve all problems. Even though money is precise, measurable, storable, and transferable, it is a very poor substitute for a friend overseas. I recently watched an American manager brush aside the proffered and necessary entré to a large Latin-American market; as with a child tying his shoes, he wanted to do it all himself. He was given the right contacts, but being independent, he chose to bypass the very people who held the key to success. A year later with import permits and approvals finally in place, the company started shipping "product," only to find itself undersold by another American competitor who had stood by and watched while the technical legal clearances were arranged. The competitor spent his time developing local contacts where it counted. Defeats of this sort in the world marketplace could have been avoided if the American manager had known and accepted two things: first, that all markets are local and, second, that it is not only all right, but essential, to admit that one does not know all there is to know about all the markets in the world.

If this had been taken into account, not only would the product have been placed in the right hands and distributed through the right channels, but also, had the manager taken time to establish proper human relationships, his accounts would have been safe.

Once while visiting in Tokyo, Professor Van Zandt told me of accounts lost because of price, but these same accounts eventually returned to the fold because his U.S. competitors were unaware of the great value placed on human relationships which Van Zandt understood so well. Now that the SEC has seriously curtailed American business in the spending of stockholder's dollars to *buy* friends and influence, I predict that American business may eventually be coerced into doing what it should have done all along—lay greater emphasis on human relationships abroad.

Friendship

Latin-American businessmen are often mystified by the American penchant for *contracts.* Their feeling is that if you have to force someone to abide by the letter of contract you have lost the game in the first inning. It is my understanding that the same could be said of Japan where *friendships* are also valued highly and *a man's word is his bond.* At this point one would normally go into an analysis of friendship in different cultures. Years of research on the part of distinguished scientists like Kurt Lewin, as well as my own studies, reveal that Americans place a much more "temporary" value on friendship than most of the rest of the world. We are situational in our friendship, whereas in many parts of the world friends and relatives are the only anchor to windward that exists in the stormy seas of life.

For those of you who may be wondering how to learn to be effective in another culture it is important to keep the following in mind. For those cultures where friendships and human relations are paramount, it is much easier to learn what you need to know about the culture from a friend; he can tell you things that others won't. Moreover, he will be more inclined to understand and accept your cultural idiosyncracies. This is illustrated by the case of engineer "Y," an American from the "Bible Belt," who was very successful even though he violated "American" stereotypes of the local rules of conduct. Because of his small town background he had grown up in an atmosphere of close relationships with others. Since friendships at home were a way of life, he and his wife were driven to find the friends they needed overseas. In the Middle East, where I knew them, "Y" had an aversion to the local cuisine and could only eat food prepared by his wife. According to the conventional American wisdom this could have created problems, but instead, the people understood and allowances were made. No one to my knowledge ever took offense because of this man's idiosyncrasies. After all, this man was their friend and, as their friend, he would not offend them. They also understood how he could have taboos about food.

This is just one example of how simplistic formulas about how to behave overseas are much less effective than the proper selection of overseas personnel, with special attention to matching people with the demands of the job. Years ago I did some research on friendship using United States, Latin-American, Arab, Indian, and African subjects. There had been complaints about how Americans behave, often picking people up and then putting them aside just as quickly. This practice mystifies most foreigners and leaves them with an empty, hurt feeling. According to my U.S. research subjects, Americans have several grades of "friends" ranging from "barely-known" through "acquaintances," "close friends," and finally "best friends." When I asked Americans to rank their friends, few had any trouble doing so. When I asked how much money they would lend different categories of friends, this did not prove difficult to talk about either. Furthermore, I found that an American can draw lines quite readily between categories of friends according to how much of his true self he would reveal. But, without exception, all my foreign subjects had trouble with these distinctions. Many foreign people do not distinguish degrees of friendship. In many countries either you are a friend or not, and the obligations that accompany friendship apply to all friends. Friendship in other parts of the world is frequently treated as something akin to being a member of the family with all that that implies. This permits one to have friends whom one likes more than others, but it does not exempt one from the obligations of friendship. People in other countries take obligations to friends seriously. Americans are fixated on the degree to which they *like* someone. Likes and dislikes can be transitory. Also, we tend to like people who are "on the team." But, as we all know, situational loyalties can also be ephemeral.

What does all this mean for the prospect of improving human relations overseas? First, like alcoholics, we have to admit that there is a problem. Unless this admission is made, there is little that anyone can do. For many years Americans have been the richest, most technologically advanced people in the world; it is this very emphasis on technology that has caused us to underemphasize human relationships. As a result, we are underdeveloped in our capacity to experience our own feelings and unskilled in many of our relationships with others. *Alienation* and *anomie* are two words one hears often these days. Widespread interest in encounter groups, primal therapy, Erhard Seminars Training, Esalen, Arica, Silva Mind Control, transcendental meditation, and transactional psychology are all evidence of the feeling of emptiness which afflicts many Americans. While these manifestations are basically narcissistic in character, they do reflect our own recognition of a need to relate to each other more meaningfully. A moment's thought reveals that one is nothing without other people, and that the underlying motivation behind most, if not all, our acts is a desire for meaningful communication and closeness to others. This brings us back to the point made at the beginning, namely, that life is first, last, and always made up of human relationships.

What U.S. Companies Need To Know

Now, as to what kinds of things American business should be aware of when setting up operations abroad, the list is extensive, in fact, almost inexhaustible. Most companies start with technical, legal, political, and economic inputs. This information is available upon request from our various government agencies. However, there is a different kind of information that is NOT generally available because people take it for granted, and it is seldom put into words. Any check list for business overseas should include information on these key points:

1. *Information chains and networks:* Who should business pay attention to and what kinds of information should be taken seriously? What should be ignored? Where are the points of entry into information networks? It is difficult to overemphasize the importance of adequate knowledge of information flow. Where does it go? How does it reach influential people? How is it evaluated?

2. *Bargaining process and procedures:* Many Americans don't really

like to bargain. Given their druthers, they would rather state their price on a take it or leave it basis. Therefore, these American businessmen must first overcome their own reluctance to bargain, and then accept the fact that there are *many different bargaining patterns* that must be mastered. For this, a local expert is needed.[1]

3. *Meaning of agreements:* When is an agreement not an agreement? All over the world there are local definitions of what constitutes a binding agreement. Americans are used to relying on written contracts and tend to insist on them. However, there are times when this need to insure performance through written contracts is not only unnecessary, but it can be taken as an insult.

4. *How to sell:* In many countries marketing information and sales practices differ widely from the American models and deserve special study.

5. *The grammar of time:* Attitudes toward deadlines, waiting periods, appointments, and time required for a relationship to develop are all different around the world. They constitute a special language which must be mastered.

6. *How to handle local bureaucracies:* This is difficult enough at home. Abroad it can be horrendous. With the proper help, however, most bureaucracies *are* manageable.

7. *What constitutes control of a company?* Increasingly, countries are demanding that 50 percent or more of the ownership be in local hands. But, this does not necessarily mean local control. For example, in some countries, the right to name the chief executive constitutes control.

8. *What constitutes friendship?* What are the expectations and obligations of friendship? As stated earlier, Americans are apt to be deficient in this area, and they undervalue the critical nature of friendship which is often the pivot around which all other matters revolve.

For all of the above information, American business should consult an expert and learn to work with him. Indeed, choosing the right advisor may be the single most important decision any business can make.

In order to improve human relations abroad we must begin at home. This means reordering our priorities, looking beyond the things that we acquire, and asking ourselves whom are we trying to impress?

It means admitting that at times we may have a problem, and that there are some things that other people of the world can teach us about how to be a friend. At the risk of sounding manipulative — which I do not intend and would not recommend — some of our countrymen will discover that as they learn how to be friends, not only will they enjoy life more, but they will also be much more effective in their jobs both at home and overseas. I do not want to give the impression that this is easy. It is not. In fact, one of the most difficult tasks in the world is to dissolve the hidden and frequently unconscious barriers that separate oneself from others. Remember, most of us are preoccupied with controlling our inputs, and we pay very little attention to changing the hidden reference signals inside ourselves that make us squirm when other people don't behave as we feel they should.

All of this implies that we should put other people on the same level as ourselves and that we take them very, very seriously. Are we up to this most difficult, most rewarding, most important task? The answer lies in each and every one of us. We might just succeed in the twenty-three years that are left in this millenia, but to do so, we will have to change our priorities.

NOTES

[1] Edward T. Hall, *The Silent Language,* (Doubleday-Anchor, 1959) provides further details.

TWO

An Overview of Europe, The Middle East and Africa

Sir James Lindsay

Currently he is Director of International Programmes at the Administrative Staff College at Henley-on-Thames in England. He joined the College in 1969 and was appointed to his present position the following year. Created a Knight Bachelor by the Queen of England in 1966, he is a Director of Nimbus International Business Development, Ltd. and a fellow of the British Institute of Management and the Institute of Marketing.

Lindsay has had a distinguished career in business. He started out with the Metal Box Company in London in 1934 and served with this firm in India from 1937-1969. His last position was Chairman of The Metal Box Co. of India, Ltd.

In addition to his business responsibilities with Metal Box, he also served as a director or chairman of three other firms in India, and as President of the Calcutta Management Association, of the All India Management Association, of the Associated Chambers of Commerce and Industry of India and as a governing body member of many professional and advisory bodies.

My objective is to persuade you to cast your minds forward in time towards the end of the twentieth century and to see if, between us, we

Many of the tables within this chapter have been updated to reflect the recent publication of the 1977 World Bank Atlas.

can discover worthwhile clues to the prospects in store for Europe, the Middle East, and Africa. This is such a tremendous segment of the globe (about one-third of the world's people and half its income), that to cover the ground I must necessarily take a broad brush approach, communicate almost telegraphically, and ask you to accept much approximation, condensation, and generalization, leaving detail to be discussed during question periods.

I speak as a businessman who has always believed that today's decisions should be influenced by—not necessarily overridden by—a vision of the future, because how we handle the short and the medium term must determine, to an important degree, our future prospects. Thus I begin with an examination of present situations because a correct understanding of what is happening right now is essential if we are to achieve insights into the future. Indeed, the only point of a businessman's forward probing into time is to discover guidelines which will usefully influence present strategies, and the starting point in formulating strategy is what the *real* situation is now at this moment.

A GEOPOLITICAL OUTLINE

An important point to notice is that the *major economic divisions of the world are horizontal* as is indicated in Fig. 2.1. The rich live in the north temperate belt between the 30th and 60th parallels: North America, Western and Eastern Europe, USSR and Japan; the world's poor live between the 30th parallel north and the 30th parallel south. This is where all the developing countries are located, with the significant exception of China. As we shall see in detail in a moment, while most of the *purchasing power* is in the *north*, the great majority of the *people* are in the south. The southern temperate zone, in latitudes 30 to 60 degrees south, contains useful "pockets" of affluence, e.g., southern Australia, New Zealand, Argentina, and South Africa, but it is unlikely to develop any great market, or any great power-base because the region consists mainly of sea, and you need land on which to grow significant masses of population. According to World Bank figures published in 1977 and shown in Table 2.1, the developed countries of the world's temperate zones have 80 percent of the world's GNP, but only 29 percent of its people—meaning that the 2900 odd million people

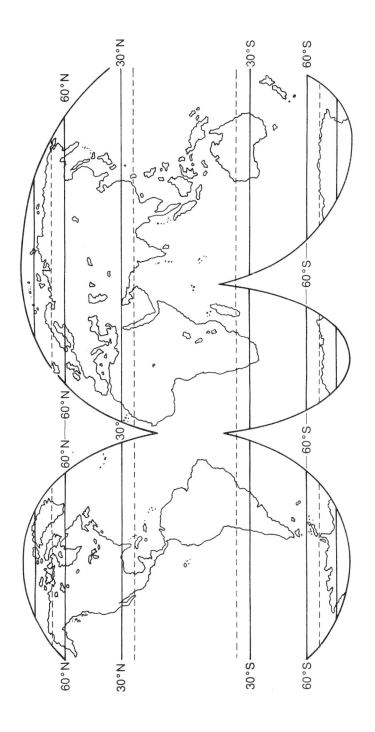

Fig. 2.1 Major Economic Divisions of the World

who constitute 71 percent of the world's population are expected not only to survive, but to develop, on 20 percent of the world's income, with some, but not very much, help from their friends.[1]

Table 2.1   Worldwide GNP and Population, 1976

		PEOPLE	GNP in U.S. $	
		(million)	$ Total (billion)	Per Capita
The Industrialized Temperate Zones	North America	238	$1872	$7866
	Japan	113	553	4910
	Oceania	20	99	4950
	Europe Less USSR	517	2152	4162
	Total	888	4676	$5266
	USSR	257	708	2760
	Industrial World Total	1145(29%)	$5384(80%)	$4702
The Developing South	Middle East	80	$ 176	$2200
	Rest of Asia Less Japan	2042	620	333
	Latin America	326	357	1095
	Africa	423	179	417
	Third World Total	2871(71%)	$1332(20%)	$ 461
	Grand Total	4016(100%)	$6716(100%)	$1668

SOURCE: *World Bank Atlas, 1977.*

We are all aware of the great gap between the living standards in the temperate zones of the world and those in the other zones. It is not very profitable to talk about closing this gap; it will never be closed. However, we should today speculate on the extent to which the more grinding levels of poverty may be eliminated, because it is of great humanitarian, as well as of business interest, that they should be.

THE NORTHERN POWERS AND THEIR SPHERES OF INFLUENCE

Before we deal with trade let us consider power. In contrast to the horizontal economic divisions I have described, *the political divisions of the northern powers are delineated vertically.* By moving down the map, south of the 30th parallel, their natural geopolitical spheres of interest can be identified as follows: south of the *United States* is Latin America; south of *Western Europe* and the *Eastern Bloc* are the Middle East and Africa; and south of *China* and *Japan* are Vietnam, Southeast Asia, Indonesia, and Australia.

The power potential of these north-north countries, as they are sometimes called, is illustrated by the fact that whenever they (however rarely) agree unanimously amongst themselves, what they say goes; in effect they then comprise a world directorate. It is not entirely coincidental that the Security Council of the UN consists of them. As political and economic power follow one another, so the ideological tendencies of the dominant northern economies gravitate downwards into the *southern* "backyards" which are their spheres of influence. Hence the Monroe Doctrine and its effect on Latin-American politics; hence the unwavering Chinese position in the Vietnam war, and the USSR's particular interest in the Middle East and Africa.

EUROPE AND ITS VERTICAL "BACKYARD"

By now it must be clear that the region with which we are concerned constitutes a logical geopolitical segment of the world, comprising OECD Europe, the USSR, and Eastern Europe as the northern (or north-north) elements while the south is made up of the Middle East, North Africa, sub-Saharan tropical Africa, and temperate southern Africa. In Europe the populations of the east and west are almost exactly balanced. The population of the EEC is virtually the same as the USSR's and, further, the population of the rest of Western Europe equates that of the remaining Eastern European countries. The major trade flows of the region are to and from Western Europe, North America, and Japan, and there is a heavy dependence on the Middle East for oil. Table 2.2 shows the total size of the market and illustrates

Table 2.2   Eurafrica/Middle East GNP and Population, 1976

	Population (million)	GNP $ (billion)
N—N TEMPERATE		
Western Europe		
EEC	259	$1402
Rest	127	412
	386	$1814
Eastern Europe		
USSR	257	708
Rest	131	338
	388	$1046
THE SOUTH		
Middle East	80	$ 176
North Africa	80	57
Tropical Africa	285	78
	445	$ 311
S—S TEMPERATE		
South Africa	26	35
Other	32	9
	503	$ 355
Total Market	1277	$3215

SOURCE: *World Bank Atlas,* 1977.

the disparity in economic strength between the north and south. Including the USSR, 774 million people in Eastern and Western Europe command a total GNP of $2860 billion, whereas the 503 million people in the south of the region earn a mere $335 billion. The northern portion of the south is infinitely richer than the tropical African region. In the Middle East and North Africa 160 million souls command a GNP of $223 billion. Even with Nigeria included, tropical Africa's 285 million subsist on less than a third of that, i.e. on $274 per annum per person (see Table 2.1). The real picture of poverty is clear from Table 2.3. This information is summarized in Table 2.4.

Table 2.3   Eurafrica/Middle East: The Rich and the Poor Countries

PER CAPITA IN 1973		EURAFRICA/MIDDLE EAST: The Rich and the Poor
VERY POOR (Less than $200)	Middle East (1)	Yemen Arab Republic and Yemen People's Democratic Republic
	Africa (16)	Benin, Barundi, Central African Republic,* Chad, Ethiopia, Gambia, Mali, Niger, Rwanda, Sierra Leone, Somalia, Sudan, Tanzania, Togo, Uganda, Upper Volta, Zaire
POOR ($200/499)	Europe (1)	Albania
	Middle East (2)	Jordan, Syria
	Africa (21)	Angola, Botswana, Cameroon, Cape Verde Is., Congo, Egypt, Guinea-Bissau, Ivory Coast, Liberia, Mauritania, Mauritius, Morocco, Mozambique, Nigeria, San Tome, Senegal, Seychelles, Swaziland, Tunisia, Zambia, Zimbabwe (Rhodesia)
MIDDLING ($500/1999)	Europe (7)	Bulgaria, Greece, Hungary, Portugal, Spain, Turkey, Yugoslavia
	Middle East (6)	Bahrain, Iran, Iraq, Lebanon, Oman, Saudi Arabia
	Africa (4)	Algeria, Ceuta, Gabon, South Africa
RICH ($2000/4999)	Europe (11)	Austria, Benelux, Czechoslovakia, Finland, France, German DR, Italy, Norway, Poland, United Kingdom, USSR
	Middle East (2)	Israel, Libya
VERY RICH ($5000 and over)	Europe (3)	Denmark, Sweden, Switzerland
	Middle East (3)	Kuwait, Qatar, United Arab Emirates

SOURCE: *World Bank Atlas,* 1975.
*Now Empire

Table 2.4   Eurafrica/Middle East: 1973 Comparisons of GNP Per Capita

	POOR AND VERY POOR $0 to $499	MIDDLING $500 to $1999	RICH AND VERY RICH $2000 to $4999 and over
GNP (per Capita ave.) Europe less USSR ($2990)	1	3	14 $\neq$
USSR ($2030)			
Middle East ($1080)	3 ϕ	6	5 $\neq$
Africa ($290)	37 *	4	1

SOURCE: *World Bank Atlas*, 1975.

*   17 of these are *very poor: GNP/capita under $200.*
ϕ 2 of these are *very poor: GNP/capita under $200.*
$\neq$ 3 of these are *very rich: GNP/capita over $5000.*

Trade

Before talking about trade with the Communist or the developing countries, we should make it clear that the *major* flows of trade *and* investment all happen across the temperate regions, notably within the trading system which governs the OECD world, namely GATT, the General Agreement of Tariffs and Trade, and within the autarkic— relatively self-sufficient—systems of Comecon and China. (Comecon, or the Council for Mutual Economic Assistance [CMEA], consists of the USSR, Eastern Europe less Albania and Yugoslavia, plus Cuba and Outer Mongolia.) The world's export figures for 1976 in Fig. 2.2 illustrate this.

This diagram reflects the fact that by far and away the biggest of the United States customers, *outside* the U.S.A. (the largest U.S. markets are within the country), are the temperate zone countries of the

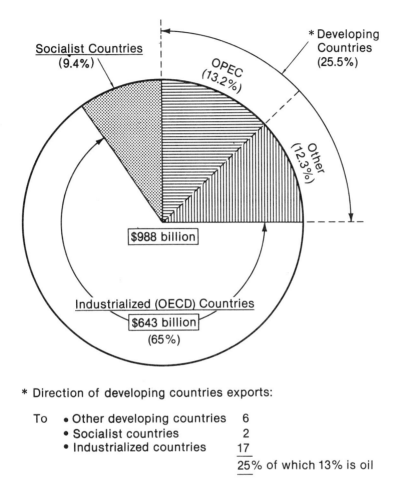

* Direction of developing countries exports:

To • Other developing countries   6
      • Socialist countries   2
      • Industrialized countries   17
                                  25% of which 13% is oil

Sources: UN Yearbook of International Trade Statistics, 1976.
            The OPEC figure is from *The Economist Diary* for 1978.

Fig. 2.2 World Exports: 1976

OECD; well behind in importance (except for Middle-East oil) are the
mixed-economy developing countries and the Communists. But will
the GATT (horizontal) system of trading hold up against western protectionist and isolationist tendencies and the vigorous onslaught of

Japanese competition? Japanese exports in 1976 are expected to be up some three and one-half compared with 1970. Thanks to Japanese vigor and to the effectiveness of their nontariff barriers to imports, their visible trade surplus in 1976 may be as high as $10 billion. The figure for the U.S. is nearer $15 billion and the EEC $5 billion; however an unfavorable invisibles situation reduced the net balance to $5 billion for that year. [2] Already the European Economic Community pursues policies of self-sufficiency which are protectionist in their effect. America's biggest customers are *within* the United States and there is no shortage of lobbies seeking protection for numerous products that might be threatened by foreign competition.

To the extent that horizontal trading across the GATT world diminishes, the major trading powers of the north will be tempted to cultivate, and be more dependent upon, their vertical "backyards": the U.S.A. would concentrate on Latin-American trade; the Japanese on trade with Australia, Indonesia and Southeast Asia; and Western Europe on the Middle East and Africa. These "backyards" are not completely fenced in — Cuba and Outer Mongolia are in Comecon, the Chinese have massive projects in Africa, the Japanese and the Germans have for many years been active in Brazil, and the U.S.A. has that longstanding and vital interest in Middle-East oil. Those of us who survive the next twenty years may well find Western Europe more inclined to look inwards and Eastern Europe more outwards. The EEC, already the world's largest trading block, will probably take in new members and extend its associate membership offering preferential trade arrangements. American business may find that to an increasing extent they will need to serve their overseas markets by overseas production and the provision of software.

The Transnationals

This presupposes that the multinational survives — and since it is an adaptive animal I believe it will — the assaults being made on it by local public opinion, home and host governments, trade unions, and the international community at large, not forgetting the international trade unions. While there is not time to deal with this large subject, I will give my view. The current vilification of the transnationals, as I suppose we must now learn to call them, reminds me of the early reaction to the wild elephant in Burma.[3] Their inclination was to drive it out or kill it. What the Burmese eventually did provides a relevant analogy: they tamed the brute and made it work for them, and even today these huge animals are using their great power and intelligence in the service of Burma. The transnationals will survive the next twenty years because they are resourceful, intelligent, and have much benevolent potential, but they *will* have to be highly adaptive. If they are, their services abroad will eventually be welcomed by host governments, but not necessarily by home country trade unions (or even by national planners) who, in the decade of job shortage ahead, will exert increasing pressure for the transnationals' funds to be invested at home.

The Markets

Having spent thirty-five years working in other people's countries, I tend to see the world in terms of markets: in the first instance, significant agglomerations of people with money to spend, whose purchasing power is a function of their number and their disposable income which grows as their countries' economies develop. The primary determinants of trade and investment, then, are, first, population size, per capita income, and per capita income growth. Secondly, the socioeconomic system which influences patterns of consumer behavior to which the businessman needs to relate his objectives, resources, and practices. Thirdly, we must not overlook value systems and influences which determine the climate in which its business operates—indeed whether or not it will be allowed to operate at all. In deciding what markets to choose in the region we are reviewing, the first set of considerations then is: (1) WHERE ARE THE PEOPLE? (2) WHAT IS THEIR PURCHASING POWER? (3) HOW IS THEIR PURCHASING POWER GROWING?

We have already established where the wealth is: the obvious first choice of markets is the affluent but highly competitive and often saturated market economies in the region's temperate zones, namely Western Europe and south Africa. Table 2.5 shows the northern temperate zone population, GNP, and growth in GNP per capita for the critical OPEC-embracing period 1970-75. Table 2.6 illustrates similar data for the southern temperate zone. The second factor in the north is

Table 2.5   Northern Temperate Zone: Population, Per Capita GNP, and Growth, 1976

| DATA | POPULATION | GNP PER CAPITA (Per Annum) | |
| | | $ | % of GROWTH 1970-75 |
COUNTRY	(million)		
Total	1991		
U.S.A.	215	$7890	1.6
Canada	23	7510	3.3
U.K.	56	4020	2
Germany	62	7380	1.9
Japan	113	4910	4
USSR	257	2760	3.1
China	836	410	5.3
Italy	56	$3050	1.7
France	53	6550	3.4
Sweden	8	8670	2.3
Switzerland	6	8880	.7

SOURCE: *World Bank Atlas,* 1977.

Table 2.6   Southern Temperate Zone: Population, Per Capita GNP, and Growth, 1976

| DATA | POPULATION | GNP PER CAPITA (Per Annum) | |
| | | $ | % of GROWTH 1970-75 |
COUNTRY	(million)		
Total	72	—	—
Argentina	26	$1550	2.9
Australia	14	6100	2.4
New Zealand	3	4250	1.5
South Africa	26	1340	1.7

SOURCE: *World Bank Atlas,* 1977.

the rapidly growing—though from a lower base—Communist markets which are particularly interested in acquiring capital goods and technology. Foreign trade is the fastest growing sector in the USSR economy: the average increase in the ninth Five Year Plan completed in

Table 2.7   Eastern Europe: Population, Per Capita GNP, and Growth, 1976

DATA COUNTRY	POPULATION (million)	GNP PER CAPITA (Per Annum) $	% of GROWTH 1970-75
Comecon	388		
USSR	257	$2760	3.1
Poland	34	2860	5.8
Romania	21	1450	10.2
East Germany	17	4220	3.7
Czechoslovakia	15	3860	3
Hungary	11	2280	3.2
Bulgaria	9	2310	3.9
Cuba*	9	860	1
Mongolia*	1.5	860	2.3
Non-Comecon	24		
Yugoslavia	22	1680	5.9
Albania	2	540	3.8

SOURCE: *World Bank Atlas,* 1977.

*Non-European members of Comecon

1975 was 11.5 percent per annum compound. The increase for 1976 was 10 percent. (See the GNP growth rates shown in Table 2.7.) As in Western Europe, Germany is the most opulent country; Romania is the poorest but fastest growing. Eastern Europe, outside the USSR, is importing some capitalist consumer goods, but the market is difficult owing to the acute shortage of hard currency. Comecon indebtedness rose $9 billion to a total of $40 billion in 1976 and the trend continues. Orders are taking longer to mature. More demands are made for "compensation trading" or "counter-trade" (meaning barter, et cetera), but there are large contracts to be had. Though not quite so slow in their dealings as the Chinese, Comecon buyers—in common with their opposite numbers in the Far East—make faithful customers who pay their bills.

Moving to the southern hemisphere, there are the developing countries which, to be worth considering commercially, must either have oil or actually *be* developing. Further, there must be sufficient population

Table 2.8   Africa: Population, Per Capita GNP, and Growth, 1976 (less OPEC)

DATA	POPULATION	GNP PER CAPITA (Per Annum)	
COUNTRY	(million)	$	% of GROWTH 1970-75
Total	429		
Egypt	38	280	1.3
Ethiopia	29	100	.4
South Africa	26	1340	1.7
Zaire	25	140	1.5
Morocco	17	540	3
Sudan	16	290	3.8
Tanzania	15	180	2.9
Kenya	14	240	2.4
Uganda	12	240	−4.5
Mozambique	9	170	−2.6
Cameroon	8	290	0.5
Ivory Coast	7	610	1.9
Rhodesia	7	550	2.8
Tunisia	6	840	6.9
Angola	5	330	3.2
Zambia	5	440	0.9
Malawi	5	140	7.0

SOURCE: *World Bank Atlas,* 1977.

if a really worthwhile market is to emerge as GNP per capita goods.

Dealing first with Africa in the 1970s, Table 2.8 presents overall a dismal economic picture. Except for the north, Nigeria, and southern Africa, it is characterised by preponderantly poor or very poor countries and low growth. In non-OPEC sub-Saharan Africa, the few relatively rich markets are either small (e.g. Kenya, Ivory Coast, Cameroon, and Malawi) or have been disrupted by civil war. As experience in Latin America and Nigeria has illustrated, revolutions need not have much effect on business so long as basic policies remain unchanged, and there is not too much dislocation such as there has been in Mozambique and more recently in Angola. There may be more revolutionary activity in the not-too-remote future in Namibia, in what is to become Zimbabwe as well as later in South Africa.

Table 2.9 Main OPEC Countries: Population, Per Capita GNP, Growth (1976), and Investible Surplus (1975)

INVESTIBLE SURPLUS 1975 $ (billion)	DATA COUNTRY	POPULATION 1976 (million)	GNP PER CAPITA (PER ANNUM)		
			1976 $	GROWTH 1970-75 %	1960-75 %
$ 34.3	Group 1				
21.0	Saudi Arabia	8.6	$4480	4.1	6.6
7.1	Kuwait	1.1	15480	−3.3	−2.9
4.2	United Arab Emirates	0.7	13990	1.6	13.7
1.3	Qatar	0.2	11400	−0.4	4.1
0.7	Libya	2.5	6310	3.9	10.5
$ 17.2	Group 2				
10.7	Iran	34.3	1930	13.3	8.1
4.0	Venezuela	12	2570	1.5	2.2
2.0	Iraq	11.5	1390	6.7	3.3
0.4	Algeria	16.2	990	4.3	1.8
0.1	Ecuador	7.3	640	6.1	3.4
$ 5.4	Group 3				
5.2	Nigeria	77	380	5.3	3.4
0.2	Indonesia	135	240	3.5	2.4
$ 45.7	Grand Total				

SOURCES: *World Bank Atlas,* 1977, and, for material in column 1, the British North American Committee (*1975 Report*) "Higher Oil Prices—Worldwide Financial Implications" sponsored by the British North American Research Association, the National Planning Association (U.S.A.), and the CD Howe Research Association (Canada) and published by the British North American Research Association.

The real promise, at least in the medium length of term, is to be found in the OPEC countries. The grouping in Table 2.9 requires some explanation.

Group 1: countries with high income but low capacity for absorbing their earnings, partly for cultural but chiefly for population reasons. Saudi Arabia heads this group; note the 1976 GNP per capita of $15,480 per annum in Kuwait for every man, woman, and child! Group 1 countries, having supplied all the goods and services that their domestic economies could absorb locally or from imports, were left in 1975 with an investible surplus of \$35 billion of which \$21 billion was in the hands of the Saudis.[4]

Group 2: countries with medium earnings and medium absorptive capacity. They have much larger populations than Group 1 countries. The list is headed by Iran with a GNP per capita growth rate of 8.1 percent per annum and an investable surplus in 1975 of \$10.7 billion.

Group 3: consists of two countries with very large populations and therefore high absorptive capacities but with relatively low oil revenues. Even so, Nigeria in 1975 had an investable surplus of \$5.2 billion.

Climate for Investment

Markets abroad are serviced by exports or international production, according to the balance of advantage in each situation. Most transnational companies prefer to build up the economies of scale which are possible when production is concentrated in a single country, preferably their own country, serving overseas markets as far as possible by exports. The competitive need to be closer to markets, to sources of cheaper labor or raw materials, or to get around protective duties and quotas, will trigger production abroad, usually as the second preference. Where it is impracticable to supply markets with goods, for example when the capital cost of setting up plants in locations all over the world is beyond a company's means—as it is in the case of the float glass process, or where the purchasers are chronically short of hard currency, as in Comecon countries, companies will sell technology as a final option. (However, the wisdom of Fiat's equipping the Russians and the Poles to undercut them by selling Lada or Polski Fiats in Italy's principal foreign markets remains open to serious question.)

Since production abroad, in wholly or partly owned subsidiaries or joint ventures, is an important alternative to exporting, let us consider the climate that business requires for such ventures. In a nutshell, the host country should be prepared to: (1) let you *earn* profits, on the basis of equitably shared benefits; (2) allow you to *keep* a reasonable fraction of them; and (3) permit you to *remit* most of what you are allowed to keep.

One of the first 'climatic' requirements frequently quoted is that the country should be "politically stable."[6] I wonder how valid it really is and if the countries attracting foreign investment today *are* all that stable politically. What about Brazil, Nigeria, Hong Kong, Singapore, South Korea, Taiwan, Iran, and Indonesia? *They are growing fast,* but what else do they have in common? It seems to me that there are two ongoing policies that their governments maintain:

1. They give a fair wind to private enterprise, local as well as foreign — if the capitalists of the host country are badly treated, foreign capital is unlikely to fare better in the long run;
2. There is a recognition that big money, i.e., good profits, made in a country of have-nots will cause discontent. Therefore, a strong law and order situation — in blunter terms, an effective coercive capability — is required to contain disaffection. In our region, consider how effective the police are in Iran and how strong the military are in Nigeria.

What international business needs is not so much political stability as *policy* stability. So long as revolutions are not accompanied by changes of policy, business can survive. But investment calculations can be completely thrown when tax rates are drastically varied from year to year, when retroactive imposts are applied, or when, having innovated a fast-growing line, new regulations prevent the firm from expanding its capacity to meet the burgeoning demand.

By now we have considered one or two general propositions and we have some picture of the present situation in the three areas — Europe, Africa, and some of Asia — into which our region divides. Each of the areas has problems reflecting the major strategic issues faced by a world which is much more adept at solving the problems of technology than those of social and political organization. Let us now look in some detail at the different areas with a view to detecting developments.

THE CONVERGING ECONOMIC SYSTEMS OF EUROPE

Comecon is overshadowed by the USSR's superpower. The USSR's GNP per capita and that of other member states indicates that they are, by the World Bank's definition, either rich or middling rich, though none are in the very rich category. Comecon is self-sufficient in energy and raw materials but not yet in food, nor, for many years to come, likely to be self-sufficient in technology. *Western Europe* is either rich, or very rich, but lacks the political cohesion to realize its full power potential, there being a strong correlation between economic strength and political power. The *European Economic Community* (EEC) is seeking self-sufficiency in food, but is highly dependent on imported energy and strategic raw materials, almost all of which can be obtained from its southern "backyards." Although the USSR is carrying out subversive activities there, "détente" nevertheless does mean the opening up of business communications between Comecon and the outside world. Poland now sends 50 percent of its exports to capitalist countries, Romania 30 to 40 percent; East Germany exports so much to West Germany that it has been nicknamed the tenth EEC State. And some transnational investment in a Comecon country has begun, as instanced by Corning Glass's minority participation in a joint venture in Hungary.

The East-West convergence of economic interests and managerial method has its fascination. On the "Directing International Operations" program I run at Henley, The Administrative Staff College, I hear Poles and Hungarian officials expounding on profit as an essential tool for judging enterprise efficiency and testing the validity of long-term Communist investment plans; I have listened to a Polish professor explain that his subject—marketing, no less—is vital to the management of the market forces with which his country has to contend, and to the effective utilization of its scarce resources. I am not sure that many Western marketers would be too happy with his definition: "Marketing," he said, "is essentially a tool to facilitate the prevention of the accumulation of nonmoving stocks." Sadly, though Western Europe is the natural market of these countries, they are economically weak, dependent on the USSR for raw materials and energy, and are short of the hard currency they need to import Western goods and technology. Where indeed will the foreign exchange come from?

But unless the USSR breaks up—and there are some who forecast that it will—the future prospects seem to be modest.[5] For the Comecon partners, trade outside their autarkic system is for balancing shortages by imports—be they of food, consumer goods, capital equipment or technology—which have to be paid for by exports. Comecon's share of the world's industrial production is 33 1/3 percent, but it has only 10 percent of world trade. With a 1976 visible trade deficit estimated at $40 billion, Comecon scarcely has the appearance of an exciting trading partner.[6]

Twenty years hence, the USSR's population is expected to increase by one-third and, according to the Hudson Institute, its GNP should grow three- to four-fold. A manifold increase in consumption will obviously not happen within that time scale unless there is Western technical collaboration for which the Russians have the capability to pay. It would seem that[7]:

1. While its partners are economically weak, the USSR itself is both militarily and economically strong.
2. Over the next ten to fifteen years, Comecon should be capable of being self-sufficient in food as it already is in energy and raw materials.
3. The German question remains a central and unresolved issue in both Europes where, it should be noted, Germany is outstandingly the most effective economic performer in the two camps. But neither side wants the question reopened. . . .
4. Basic USSR military strategy is essentially defensive; it is about defending a substantial empire. The China-USSR rift will continue because the Soviet empire includes substantial tracts of what Peking regards as Chinese territory.

Even though the military power group in the Kremlin is strong and may have its own war games to play, it is possible—without being unduly reckless in a dangerous world—to take the optimistic view that détente and the Russian commitment to increasing domestic consumption and to freer trade will continue as an ongoing trend. Mitigating against their giving in to the autarkic isolationist temptation is the strength of the appetite at home for improved living standards. True, those have to be damped down to release exportable surpluses on the scale required. But without substantial trade, the rate of progress that Russia needs to make will be unattainable.

A Europe-wide self-sufficiency in food might be achieved; and assuming that world trade, as a whole, continues to grow, Comecon-EEC cooperation should develop, with the western partners offering technological goods and software in exchange for oil from Russia and coal from Poland as before World War II.

THE EEC, EUROPEAN INTEGRATION, AND POWER

Western Europe's problem is lack of the political will, determination, and credibility that will give it world-power status reflecting its economic strength.[8] In the long term, political power, prestige, military capability, nuclear status, prosperity, and the capacity to offer development aid all find their basis, and their limitation, in the country's gross national product. The most decisive economic factors in the make-up of GNP usually quoted in this context are size of population, production per capita, iron and steel production, energy availability, nuclear capability and computer density. This is not to suggest that the course of the world is finally, and exclusively, dependent on a material concept of society. Quite to the contrary, history shows that at critical moments in war, the moral fibre of the nation, its determination, capacity for hard work, and willingness to sacrifice may well decide the outcome. These same qualities produce GNP growth. Nor is its political power necessarily in phase with a country's economic strength. Consider, for example, the case of the United States before World War II and that of West Germany after it: then, the political influence of these countries in no way matched their economic strength. On the other hand, Britain between the wars continued to exercise greater political power than its diminishing economic condition justified. While economic strength does not guarantee commensurate political influence, that is likely to come about over time, and it is certainly an indispensable precondition of power. The figures in Table 2.10 show the potential power of the EEC alongside the USSR and the other countries moving towards superpower status.

It can be seen from Tables 2.10 and 2.11 that the population, steel production, and—above all—the GNP figures for the year 2000 may take Japan and, probably, China (which is, and will be, self-sufficient in energy), into the superpower league. The same could be said of Europe: if only it were united, Europe's political strength could be superior to that of the USSR. But without close political integration, the individual member countries will lack the collective will to achieve an audible voice in a world of giants. As a result, the power of Europe would not be much greater than that of its strongest member, notably West Germany, whose GNP is unlikely to be more than $850 billion

Table 2.10 Population and GNP: 1976 to 2000

DATA	POPULATION (million)		GROSS NATIONAL PRODUCT (U.S. $ billion)	
COUNTRY	1976*	2000+	1976*	2000
China	836	1170/1500	$ 343	$ 715/1000
Japan	113	130	553	1700/2000≠
U.S.A.	215	270/ 280	1698	2700/3700≠
USSR	251	330	708	1500/2170≠
EEC	258	280	1402	2500/3070+

For the years 1976-2000 some detailed figures are:

West Germany	62	70	$389	$850+
U.K.	56	60	201	520+

SOURCES: * *World Bank Atlas*, 1977.
+   Hudson Institute/OECD. See Mesarovic and Pestel, "Mankind at the turning point" in the Second Report of the Club of Rome, Hutchinson of London, 1975.
≠ Author's own figures. The Hudson Institute OECD GNP totals for these countries quoted by Mesarovic et al. seem unrealistic viz. Japan 2000 $2200/$3500 billion and USSR 2000 $1500/$2170. So, too, does the US 2000 GNP bracket of $3760/4000 billion; it is unlikely to be higher than $3700.

Table 2.11 Selected Steel Production 1973-2000: Some Major Countries and the EEC

DATA	STEEL PRODUCTION (million tons)	
COUNTRY	1973	2000
China	25	70
Japan	115	180 plus
U.S.A.	136	180
USSR	131	180
EEC	150	180

SOURCE: J. G. de Beus, "Europe among the Super-Powers in the Year 2000," New Europe (Summer 1974), pp. 29-41.

by the end of the century, compared with the lower bracket figures for Japan ($1700 billion) and the U.S. ($3760 billion).

European integration can move in two directions: laterally, according to the Treaty of Rome, whereby *all* European countries genuinely practicing parliamentary democracy may join the EEC communities; and in depth from a customs union, towards economic union and eventually to full-blooded political union.[9] These are conflicting directions, in that the first makes the second more difficult to achieve. Indeed at this moment, the European Commission, notwithstanding the Rome Treaty commitments, is being very cautious about expansion. There is a dilemma concerning the fringe countries, recently escaped from totalitarian regimes and which the West wishes to keep out of the Soviet orbit: Greece, Spain, and Portugal are cases in point, as well as the Yugoslavs. These countries may be entitled to join but they will be exceedingly difficult to accommodate within the EEC framework because they have weak economies and are politically shaky. In any case, the European Commission's bureaucracy and the slowness of its consensus-style of decision-making will be even more cumbersome if the number of countries enlarges. And the very different characteristics of the new members will make political integration that much more difficult to achieve. There is an influential view to the effect that there are circumstances in which the EEC *could* be a superpower by the year 2000; the underlying assumptions being that the EEC would have to:

1. *Weather the current economic hurricane,* avoiding both import controls and a reversion to economic nationalism;
2. *Survive the possible emergence of popular front governments* containing Communist ministers, e.g., in Italy or France;
3. *Not be obliged to compound politically* with the USSR through failure of will to provide for its own defense and consequent lack of U.S. military support;
4. *Have a common decision-center* with a directly elected parliament which would cover all spheres of activity including defense;
5. *Accept that it might be joined by Norway* (because Denmark is in), *Spain, Portugal, Switzerland*—which is now questioning the long-term value of neutrality—and Greece (to whom promises have been made), to constitute a union of fourteen countries in all;
6. *Be responsible for its own defense,* in alliance with the U.S., by the late 1980s.

7. *Be associated with five more countries:* Austria, Finland, Sweden, Turkey, Malta; and
8. *Have economic links* with at least the forty-nine Lomé Convention signatories.

Another argument suggests that if there is no political union, the European Economic Community will eventually be disrupted because:

1. Without collaboration between member states in military matters, there will be no common defense, and the U.S. will lose heart and withdraw its support, particularly if there are Communists in Western European governments;
2. Left-wing governments would then seek to make individual deals with the USSR;
3. The mixed economies would cease to be, and the continuing European entity would be an enlarged Comecon, conceivably a Comecon with more respect for capitalist values.

The debate is an uncomfortable one: west European cooperation — close enough to amount to political union — is unlikely to develop within the required time scale, that is unless the countries of Western Europe are confronted with a grave common peril sufficiently overt to be perceived as such. Who was it that suggested that the arrival in, say, California of a few "sci-fi" creatures from outer space would result in the formation of a world government within a week?

WEST ASIA — THE MIDDLE EAST

The part of the region of greatest importance to the United States is west Asia, otherwise known as the Middle East, because the good Lord when resourcing that part of the world added oil to the camels and the profusion of sand, and the United States, like the rest of the Western world — only more so because of her vast domestic resources — is hooked on energy. The Middle East produces a high percentage of the U.S.A.'s oil imports and possesses 70 percent of the earth's known oil reserves as is apparent in Table 2.12.[10] This important corner of Asia has a population of 79 million, consisting of 3.6 million nonfeudal Jews in Israel, 31 million feudal non-Arab Muslims in Iran, and 44.5 million Arab Muslims in the Asian states as mentioned in Table 2.13. There

Table 2.12   Middle-Eastern Oil-Producing Countries Ranking in Order of Certain Characteristics

OIL RICHNESS[1]		SIZE OF OIL REVENUE[2]	DOMESTIC FUND REQUIREMENT[3]		SURPLUS FUNDS[4]
Saudi Arabia	138	Saudi Arabia	Iran	26.6	Saudi Arabia
Kuwait	65	Iran	Algeria	13.8	Libya
Iran	65	Kuwait	Kuwait	0.6	Kuwait
Libya	30	Libya	Iraq	9.1	Iraq
Iraq	29	Iraq	Abu Dhabi	0.2	Abu Dhabi
Abu Dhabi	21	Abu Dhabi	Libya	1.9	Iran
Algeria	15	Algeria	Saudi Arabia	7.5	Algeria

[1.] Defined as oil reserves in billions of barrels as they were known in 1972.
[2.] Based on projections over two decades of 1972 oil revenue figures.
[3.] Based on a combination of projected rise in population and modified by the propensity plus ability to consume which is a function of literacy and experience.
[4.] Based on columns 2 and 3.

are great disparities in wealth, and the area includes some very poor countries like Yemen and, as we have seen, some of the very richest.

Finance is no longer a constraint on GNP growth in the Middle East. But its abundance in no way implies that the economic and political development of the area will proceed unconstrained. Many Middle-East countries are faced with serious labor shortages; there is a very distinct disinclination in Arab countries (in Saudi Arabia in particular) for local labor to move from traditional pastoral or agricultural activities into the manufacturing sector.

Furthermore, there is no underlying unity in the area, either in regard to religious or political systems (there are kingdoms, social democracies, centrally planned, and maverick anarchist republics), or in regard to economic or social aspects.[11] The desert Arab has very little time for his ethnic brother in the coastal areas, and the Iranian Shia Muslims have little in common with the Sunni Arabs except in the possession of oil wealth. Even in the traditional regimes, such as Saudi Arabia and Oman, their conservatism reflects not—as in the West—a desire to maintain the existing distribution of moveable property, but rather continuity of the political power of the royal houses. An informed view, originating in the International Institute of Strategic

Table 2.13 Middle East: Population by Major Ethnic Groups and Political Systems, 1976

	VERY RICH (million)		MEDIUM RICH (million)	WITHOUT OIL (million)	
FEUDAL ARABS					
	Saudi Arabia	8.6		Jordan	2.8
	Kuwait	1.1			
	Oman	0.8			
	United Arab				
	Emirates	0.7			
	Bahrain	0.3			
	Qatar	0.2			
NONFEUDAL ARABS					
			Iraq	11.5	Yemen
					Arab
					Republic	6
					Lebanon	3.2
			Syria	7.6	Yemen
					People's
					Democratic
					Republic	1.7
TOTAL (in millions)	11.7		19.1	13.7	
ARABS					
Feudal		14.5			
Nonfeudal		30			
		44.5			
IRANIS					
Feudal		34			
ISRAELIS					
Nonfeudal		3.7		Feudal	48.5
				Nonfeudal	33.7
Total (in millions)		82.2		82.2	

SOURCE: *World Bank Atlas, 1977.*

Studies, stresses the real and ongoing importance of political stability to the social and political elites of the countries, and that is also important to business. But the emphasis on the "status quo" in the feudal states will widen the gaps between the poor and the rich, the powerful and the powerless, and stoke up civil disquiet. The thinly populated states of the Arabian peninsula and the lower gulf have the agonizing choice between accepting a manpower shortage as a decisive constraint on economic development or permitting a highly disruptive immigration without which development will be impeded. The manpower shortages are across the board: all these countries need managers, skilled technicians, and trained administrative personnel (with the possible exception of Iran and Kuwait); Saudi Arabia, Qatar, Oman, and the United Arab Emirates need semiskilled and unskilled workers as well.

Over the next ten to fifteen years, Iran—although better equipped to cope—may be more exposed than the Arabs to the activities of radical groups frustrated by the probable curtailment of excessively ambitious development plans. The existence of an 1800-mile frontier with the USSR will not make the situation any easier. Iran's main trading partner is Europe; indeed Europe depends heavily upon Iran for its oil supplies, so it is not surprising that the policy of the present ruler is to lean as far to the West as is consistent with the "détente" situation. But what about the future? The initial idea that the oil states might eventually achieve superpower status seems to be unlikely. It could only happen *if* the OPEC countries were able to convert their oil income into a more broad and solid-based economy and achieve a political union of the sort that we have discussed in the context of Europe. True, the binding cement of the OPEC cartel should last until the 1990s, and certainly there may be shacking up of the Egypt-Syria type, but serious political union on a large scale? Unlikely.

Over the next ten to twenty years the biggest changes may come about through domestic pressures. Huge oil wealth will bring new ways of life and impetus for structural change. Sixty percent of the inhabitants—whose numbers are expected to double by the end of the century—are governed by hereditary rulers. It will be astonishing if all the royal houses survive. Potent influences for change reside in the Arabs from nearby North Africa. Mostly nonfeudal and almost in equal numbers, they include Egyptians, Algerians, and the Libyans (the latter unpredictable at this time). An unresolved and hopefully medium-term problem for the Arabs is posed by the Israelis. With their enormous financial power, the Arabs could steadily undermine Israel. However, they would be risking an eventual nuclear response and an embroilment which could bring in the U.S.A. actively on the Israeli side. Not only the feudal Arabs would recoil from the alignment with the USSR that this prospect would promote, but also in the next decade, the nonfeudal influences in the Middle East will intensify as education and living standards are raised. At the same time the Arab-Israel conflict is likely to diminish: as the Arabs in the street and the desert become richer, their envy of Israel may begin to decline. It seems feasible that the U.S.A. and Russia will be able to reach some kind of understanding which will guarantee the frontiers and, hence, peace. If I had to bet, this is the situation on which I would put my money for the year 2000. If I were an American industrialist, I would not hesitate to invest in the Middle East, but I would resort to the old expedient of watching carefully the pay-back expectations.

ENERGY

Karl Marx's view of the inherent weakness of Western capitalism was that the monopoly of wealth by the few would result in there being insufficient consumption outlets to enable the system to keep going. The West's true weakness is that it is hooked on energy, while the majority of the energy resources are in the hands of a few nonenergy-dependent countries, who can withhold production without serious economic consequences to themselves. Before leaving the Middle East it would be well to underscore the finite aspects of its oil reserves. Some countries such as Algeria, and even Iran—Europe's main supplier—must expect to see their production declining by the mid-1980s. Clearly the West has to develop alternatives to oil as a fuel, and the Middle-East countries need to develop alternative sources of revenue.[12] The energy situation in the future now looks something like this:

Oil and Gas

1. Oil and gas go into short supply towards the end of the century: the world then begins to run out of hydrocarbons.

2. Even then the U.S.A. (despite its own huge reserves), Europe (notwithstanding the North Sea), and Japan, will be highly dependent on the Middle East unless:
   a. there are huge new discoveries or unexpected reserves from the USSR and China are released on world markets, or
   b. alternative fuels are developed.

Coal

1. Large reserves exist, much of those in Europe are in very thin seams;
2. Higher prices are needed to stimulate the mechanization of mining which, despite the unattractiveness of underground work, is held up by workers' attitudes to losing job opportunities;
3. Biochemical breakthrough is possible in terms of enzyme technology: bacteria "eat" the coal and energy is collected in the form of the gas given off. The unresolved problem worrying scientists: the exponential growth of bacteria, and doubts about what they will eat next, after all the coal has been consumed.

Solar, Tidal, Thermal, and Atomic Energy[13]

1. *Solar energy abounds:* for example two-and-a-half times the present energy requirements of Great Britain are available from solar sources, notwithstanding the gloomy climate.
2. *Solar energy from wood* is a possibility. The technology involves irrigating deserts, planting quick-growing trees for fuel—a wood crop that can be grown in eighteen months, relatively expensively, but not ridiculously so.
3. *Tidal energy* is available, e.g., in Great Britain, to the tune of ten times the country's annual requirement. Although energy is easily *produced* by solar and tidal sources (even by windmills), the problem is *how to store it.* A technological breakthrough is required; the ability to build up reservoirs of electricity would transform the interest in developing these freely and permanently available sources.
4. *Thermal energy* from land or sea water is another possibility which would benefit from such a breakthrough.
5. *Atomic energy* in presently acceptable technology is based on uranium, of which—as in the case of fossil fuels—supplies are finite. The faster-breeder reactor may be the principal known method of producing energy on the scale required by the end of

the century to support the life-style to which the West is addicted. Alas, difficult problems of *pollution control* and *security* have yet to be solved. The plutonium generated by the fast-breeders process takes 2400 years to lose half of its radioactivity. Only ten pounds of plutonium are required to construct a devastating atomic bomb, using technology which is no more complicated than that used to produce illegal heroin. Yet, a way around the appalling difficulties must be found.

That outlines the issues: action is needed to assure the continuity of our form of civilization and incidentally, to free the West from its dependence on OPEC oil. Scenarios for consideration include key areas of the Middle East being seized by an unfriendly power, supplies being withheld by the main Middle-Eastern producers, or prices being again quintupled. Building up new sources of energy which will come on stream in the nineties before one goes into short supply, demands decision-making now. While the world understandably hesitates to commit itself to the controversial fast-breeder atomic solution, this issue must now be faced. The logical alternative to grasping that horribly unpleasant nettle is to curtail energy consumption immediately, even though that solution would mean restraining, in the interests of the future, our short-term economic advancement.

The second report to the Club of Rome, "Mankind at the turning point," suggest that if alternative energy sources *are* going to develop in time, the price of oil needs to go up steadily at the rate of 3 percent per annum for fifteen years, by which time the *optimal level*, 50 percent higher at constant prices, will be reached.[14] The report concludes that the conflict between the oil producers and consumers is more apparent than real. Both will benefit by collaboration: too low a price would suit neither side, nor would too high a price. Attempts by either party to score off the other will not pay in the long run. The concept of *beneficial price range*, they claim, is valid for all finite resources—food, fertilizers, copper, et cetera—but the "optimal price" and the "proper rate of increase" will differ for each commodity and be a source of north-south controversy. This view is relevant to Africa's considerable metal and mineral resources.

THE CONTINENT OF AFRICA

Europe was first made aware of the existence of Africa in the eighth century when it was raided and invaded by the Moors from that continent. They were particularly successful in the case of Spain where they remained for seven centuries, leaving an indelible imprint on Spanish culture. While accounts of the flowering of Arab civilization in the first millenium A.D. have found their way into Western history books, much less has been said about sub-Saharan Africa's cultural accomplishments. It is not, for example, generally realized that when the Portuguese made their first tentative landfalls on the tropical west African coast, the societies they encountered there had the same basic characteristics as those of Europe and North Africa.[15] By the beginning of the sixteenth century, Africans had shown themselves as effective as the Europeans in the techniques of domestic life, cultivation, trade, social, and political organization. Kilwa (in Tanzania) could be compared with Venice as a commercial port; Timbuktu, with Rome or Paris, as a center of learning; the art of Benin and Ife ranked with any European sculpture of the time.

The early impact of Arab civilization on the sub-Saharan African societies was not a happy one. They introduced the slave trade, in which the West joined, to feed the voracious appetite for labor of the expanding plantation system. Thus the normal development of Africa's trade was completely destroyed, as was the fabric of existing society. Tropical Africa's era of medieval growth was at an end; the Dark Ages began. By the nineteenth century, being by then without social stamina or political cohesion, the Africans were virtually helpless either to resist the new European imperialism or to adopt and adapt European techniques to revolutionize their own societies. The imperial carving-up of their continent remained undisturbed until the third quarter of the twentieth century.

Independent as they now are of the metropolitan powers, the Africans live no more healthy, secure, or free lives than they did before 'Uhuru' (independence); this is notwithstanding the valiant efforts of some of their leaders who have achieved for themselves and their countries a new sense of dignity in the world. Thanks to modern communication, North Africans no longer feel emotionally cut off from the rest of Africa by the Sahara. They have a sense of belonging to the African continent, and, in common with almost all African countries, are members of the Organization for African Unity, the OAU. The main divisions of Africa fit in with the geopolitical picture I have painted: (1) the Arab north, (2) sub-Saharan tropical Africa, and (3) the temperate south. On my last count there were forty-seven independent countries in all. Nearly all are poor—seventeen of them are very poor, with only four, including South Africa, having an average GNP per capita above $500 in 1973. The south African whites are rich, and one country, Libya, is very rich. In all, the continent has 423 million inhabitants; the population could approach 800 million by the end of the century.

Except for those who are members of OPEC, it is difficult to detect much evidence of that close cooperation which is so necessary for the development of the "developing countries." The efforts to achieve re-

Table 2.14   All-Africa and African Regional Organizations: Membership Figures

ORGANIZATIONS	AFRICAN MEMBER COUNTRIES
OAU (Organization for African Unity)	46
AFDB (African Development Bank)	43
Lomé Convention	38
ACP (African Caribbean and Pacific Group)	34
CFA (Communanté Financiere Africiane)	12
African Regional Organizations	
CEAO (Communanté Economique de l'Afrique de l'Ouest)	6
Conseil de l'Entente	5
EAC (East African Community)	3
ECOWAS (Economic Community of West African States)	14
OCAM (Organisation Commune Africaine Mauricienne)	10
UDEAC (Union Douaniere et Economique de l'Afrique Centrale)	4
Total Regional	42

SOURCE: *Finance & Development* (November 1976), International Monetary Fund, Washington, D.C.

gional economic groupings of the EEC type have been up against the insuperable obstacle of a nationalism even more intense than Europe's. But Table 2.14, which sets out the organizations of which African countries are members, certainly indicates that they keep in contact.

Policy Stability in Africa

Since policy stability is so important, let us discuss it in the context of Africa, the most extreme case in our region. Here business prospects will depend to an important degree on the continent's political future, now in the melting pot. Africa falls within the geopolitical spheres of interest of the USSR's superpower and an impotent Western Europe. China has ideological motivation but is too remote from the scene to challenge the USSR, whose Cuban task force of 12 to 15 thousand well-armed troops has already been devastatingly successful in Angola. To Europeans, it seems that the U.S.A. does not view the Communist threat to sub-Saharan Africa as affecting its vital interests. What matters most to the U.S.A. is North Africa and the Middle East, particularly Saudi Arabia, her main source of imported crude oil.

One theory about Africa is that its loyalties are formed by tribal rather than ideological considerations. But please note that Angola is now officially a "Marxist-Leninist Republic." Russian advisers dominate the Ministry of Defense, Cubans virtually monopolize President Neto's personal staff, and there are treaties of military and political collaboration between Neto and Brezhnev.

Fig. 2.3 shows the extent of Soviet influence in Africa: it enables some inferences to be drawn on the areas which should be watched for changes in policy affecting private enterprise's trade and its supply lines. It indicates where there are (1) Marxist governments, (2) strong links with the USSR, (3) immediate strategic targets of the USSR, and (4) longer-term strategic targets of the USSR.

The map shows clearly the main components of Soviet strategy and achievements to date. They are relevant to business and point to the following:[16]

1. Soviet influence in the north and north-west is significant.
2. Nevertheless, the main thrust is south, with Somalia Marxist and with Tanzania and Uganda firmly in the Russian orbit.
3. Apart from what President Neto is attempting in Angola,

Fig. 2.3 Soviet Influence in Africa

Mozambique's President Machel claims to be setting up the first "fully Marxist State in Africa."

4. The Russian Navy now has port facilities from Mogadishu in Somalia (withdrawn in 1977), down the friendly Mozambique coast, around South Africa to Lobito in Angola.

5. Zimbabwe's Robert Mugabe is as committed to setting up a Marxist state as is Joshua Nkomo, Moscow's official nominee. So whatever the outcome of the present negotiations, a Marxist future for Rhodesia must be in the cards; with Zimbabwe and

Namibia "in the bag," South Africa will be completely encircled, as will Zambia and Zaire.

6. Given complete success with a strategic program of this sort, the whole of southern Africa could become a client state of the USSR.

How much would Soviet success in Africa matter to the U.S.A. and to the West at large? The answer lies in the continent's mineral wealth.[17] A Soviet expert in economic warfare has stressed the dependence of modern armaments on such raw materials as chrome, platinum, nickle, cobalt, and titanium. Any Western weakness in the source of supply of these commodities should, he believes, be exploited by the USSR. The West seems to agree with the underlying logic: at a conference in Swaziland this June, it was pointed out that the world's largest chrome, vanadium, and platinum deposits, as well as important reserves of manganese, are to be found in southern Africa. Dr. Robert Kilmarx of the Center for Strategic and International Studies at Georgetown University in Washington pointed out that in the relative power ranking of nonfuel mineral resources, South Africa was next to Australia and just below the U.S.A. and the USSR. African countries between them produce at least twenty-five metals or have reserves of them. Table 2.15 illustrates the high percentage of free world production which is located in Africa and how much of this is of interest to military strategists.

In view of the political isolation of southern Africa, the concentration of supplies in the south is especially significant. South Africa herself is an important producer of antimony, asbestos, cobalt, chrome, manganese, nickel, phosphates, platinum, uranium, vanadium, zinc, as well as diamonds and gold. Zambia and Zaire dominate with copper and cobalt; Namibia is important for copper, lead, zinc, and uranium reserves; Botswana for copper and nickel; and Zimbabwe has copper, nickel, asbestos, chrome, and lithium.

It emerges quite clearly that in strategic terms Africa, particularly southern Africa, *does* matter. That accounts, in part at least, for the longstanding efforts the USSR has been making there to assist the various freedom movements; they seem to be paying off. As a consequence, prospects for business over the next twenty years could be very bleak: there could be drastic *policy* changes following which the

Table 2.15   Africa's Mineral Wealth

	AFRICAN % OF FREE WORLD PRODUCTION	% OF U.S.A.'s REQUIREMENTS WHICH ARE IMPORTED
Strategic		
Colbalt	80	98
Chrome	40/50	91
Nickel	20 plus	—
Platinum	80	80
Titanium	20 plus	—
Other		
Aluminum	15	—
Antimony	25/30	—
Asbestos	60	—
Copper	25	—
Gold	82	—
Manganese	50	90
Uranium	25*	—
Vanadium	40	36

SOURCE: Sir Ronald Prain, address to a joint meeting of the Royal African Society and the Royal Institute of International Affairs, November 9, 1976.

* World's largest.

eventual possibilities for trade and investment could be minimal, important supply sources of strategic minerals could be eliminated, and the oil route around the Cape cut. But there is no point in prophesying per se, e.g., Cassandra's forecast of the inevitable fall of Troy. Doom, I believe, catches up only after the failure (or lack) of preventative action. I do not pretend to know the answer to the complex southern African situations, but I have indicated what may happen if they are allowed to go by default.

GENERAL COMMENTS

To sum up: The Lomé Convention and the developing USSR connection seem certain to influence African trade in a European direction.[18] It is just possible that the commodity stabilization proposals which are being pursued in the UNCTAD conferences may result in the African and other developing countries getting a fairer price for their commodities. Though this would improve their export earnings, there is no future—except conceivably for weak cartels in such products as copper, tin, and bauxite—for an OPEC type of action with other commodities. In the African countries which escape a Marxist future, there should be opportunities for the transnational prepared to enter into joint ventures to invest in key economic areas, particularly those which are agriculture related. Here the needs of these countries is great. There does, however, remain a good deal of mutual suspicion as between the transnationals and the developing countries. It is just possible that the recently set up UN Commission on Transnational Corporations will, in the long run, help both sides.[19] The dissemination of objective information could do much to allay the suspicions about the transnational companies which are largely based on a few bad cases. The emerging United Nations Code should relate to the conduct of governments, as well as to that of companies; it is unlikely to stipulate behavior for the latter which does not already characterize the practice of the leading corporations. An approach that might do much to clear the air would be for companies to accept fees paid for services rendered (as is now happening in the case of the oil industry) in preference to making equity investments in which profit is made for risk-taking. On present thinking, the developing countries would be reluctant to pay a price that reflected the true costs.

In the other scenarios I have put forward in this paper, the U.S.A. will be at some disadvantage as pertains to tariffs vis-à-vis Western European countries, and nontariff barriers may continue to obstruct trade despite the best efforts of the Tokyo and other Rounds to eliminate them. Eastern Europe's demand for American capital goods, technology, and know-how will grow, but will be contained by inability to find the hard currency to pay for these. The Middle East, still in the early stages of industrial development, has vast sums to spend on domestic requirements, so there should be good investment opportunities there, though the political risks will have to be weighed with increasing care. Western Europe, too, may continue to tempt American transnationals in the direction of external expansion though the leftward tendency—and there are likely to be moves further to the left before the political pendulum shows any sign of swinging the other way—may well discourage the U.S. investor. There may be an inwards-looking phase, a tendency for U.S. transnationals to concentrate on the United States, which is, after all, the largest market in the world for the products of American companies. Such is the dynamism of American business that, if this does happen, it is unlikely to be for long. The need for new outlets will continue to tempt U.S. companies in an external direction, including Western Europe. External trade will also be stimulated by the U.S.'s need, by the end of the century, to import 80 percent of her raw material for industrial production.[20]

CONCLUSION

My starting point indicated that since today's decisions must influence future prospects, there is a question of what the real situation is *now*. This I have reviewed, rightly or wrongly. Trying to put myself into the position of an American businessman, who is more capable of applying pressure on his government than his counterpart in Europe, I see the following key points: The need for supportive political influence to promote the closer integration of Western Europe, having in mind that political cohesion, added to economic strength, will build up both a good trading partner and a valuable ally, and that a more firmly integrated Europe will be able to exert a stronger influence, vertically, particularly in Africa, with benefit to the free world by: (1) affecting the flow of Africa's strategic mineral wealth; (2) maintaining and developing communications, trade, investment, and technology flows with the African and the Middle-Eastern countries; (3) helping the development processes in those countries.

It has been stated that the American expression of interest in the African continent, particularly in Angola, Mozambique, Rhodesia, South Africa and now the Horn of Africa (Ethiopia, Somalia, et cetera) is rather late: a self-interested gesture triggered by the Communist successes both in the South and the North. There may be some truth in this. Personally, I believe the West has some time, but not much. The whole of Africa is not impressed with Russian financial and technical aid. And they will, for example, not be unaware of India's experiences, where the financial terms have been harsh, and the technological inputs poor. My hope is that the new administration in the United

States will: (1) encourage American joint ventures in the African continent, so that there not only is, but can be seen to be, participation between Africa itself and the free world at large, and (2) encourage the EEC not only to develop economic unity, but also the "will to live" as a political, and eventually a military entity. In this context, any talk of isolationism or military withdrawal from Europe is a counsel of despair.

NOTES

1. *World Bank Atlas, 1977,* published by the World Bank; see also *OECD Member Countries Statistics,* 1976.

2. Japanese trade deficit figures from GATT furnished by Professor T. Mende, previously advisor to the Secretary General of UNTAD. The export figures are confirmed by The Economist Diary for 1978 published in London by *The Economist* newspaper.

3. See the United Nations study of multinationals: statement by P. deSeynes, Under Secretary-General for Economic Affairs. See also United Nations, ECOSOC, "Draft Programme of Work on the Full Range of Issues Relating to Transnational Corporations" in *Report of the Secretary-General* (EC-10/2), February 28, 1975; see UN Center on Transnational Corporations publication E/C 10/18, 1977, "Material Relevant to the Formalization of a Code of Conduct."

4. Sperry Lea: *Higher Oil Prices — Worldwide Financial Implications, British North American Committee Report* (Washington, D.C.: National Planning Association, 1975), p. 38.

5. See the dissident Andrei Almarik's paper, "Will the Soviet Union Survive Until 1984?" quoted in *The Economist,* 24 July 1976, p. 14.

6. See Litvaic and Banting, "A Conceptual Framework for International Business Arrangements" in *Marketing and the New Science of Planning* (Fall 1968) Conference Proceedings of the American Marketing Association, pp. 460-67.

7. Lord Gladwin, "Europe in 1986." He is a member of the European parliament of the European Communities (EEC).

8. J. G. deBeus, "Europe among the Super-Powers in the Year 2000," *New Europe* (Summer 1974), pp. 29-41. He was the Netherlands' ambassador to Spain. Other works consulted include "Britain in the Eighties: Detailed Forecast to 1985," The

Henley Centre for Forecasting (London, 1975); "Europe Plus Thirty Report," Commission of the European Communities (Brussels, 1975); "Framework Forecasts for the EEC Economies," The Henley Centre for Forecasting (London, 1976).

9. Richard Mayne, Information and Press Office (London) of the Commission of the European Communities.

10. N. A. White, Energy Adviser to the Board of Hambros Bank, London, previously with Shell International as chief executive, New Enterprises Division.

11. See "Future Political Patterns in the Middle East," by Ian Smart, Deputy Director, International Institute of Strategic Studies, in *The World Today* (London: The Royal Institute of International Affairs, July 1976). See also "Middle East Economic Prospects: Forecasts to 1985 (London: The Henley Centre for Forecasting, 1975).

12. "Mankind 2000," ed. R. Jungk and J. Galtung, International Peace Research Institute, Oslo (London: Allen & Unwin, 1971).

13. *The Economist,* 25 September 1976, pp. 100-01. See also Michael Kenward, "The Sun, the Waves and the Wind," in *New Scientist* (1976), and "Future World Trends," discussion paper published by the Cabinet Office (London, 1976).

14. Mihajlo Mesarovic and Eduard Pestel, "Mankind at the Turning Point," Second Report to the Club of Rome (London: Hutchinson & Co., 1975).

15. John Hatch, *Post-War History of Africa* (London: Methuen, 1976).

16. Lord Chalfont, journalist, previously Minister of State, British Government Foreign and Commonwealth Office, and defense correspondent of *The Times,* in *The Times,* 22 November 1976.

17. Sir Ronald Prain, "Metal and Africa: Economic Power in an International Setting" (An address to a joint meeting of the Royal African Society and the Royal Institute of International Affairs, Chatham House, London, November 9, 1976).

18. Hajo Hasenpflug, "The Convention of Lomé—Towards a New International Cooperation?" in *Intereconomics* 6 (1975).

19. Refer to studies cited in note [3] above.

20. Mesarovic and Pestel, "Mankind at the Turning Point."

REFERENCES

Cohen, Michael A. "Cities in Developing Countries: 1975-2000." Based on *World Bank Staff Working Paper No. 209*. Washington, D.C.: Bank Publications Office.

Gordon, J. King. "The New International Economic Order." Ottawa: *Canadian Institute of International Affairs*, 1976.

Mende, Tibor. *From Aid to Recolonization — Lessons of a Failure*. London: Howrays, 1973.

Pearson, L. B. *Partners in Development: the Pearson Report*. London: Pall Mall Press, 1967.

Schumacher, E. F. *Small Is Beautiful*. London: Blond & Briggs, 1973.

Streeten, P. *Trade Strategies for Development*. London: Macmillan, 1973.

United Nations. *Urban-Rural Projections from 1950-2000. 1974.*

vanEeden, J. J. "South Africa's Urban Dilemma." In *To the Point*, International Issue, London, 23 August 1976.

Rostow, W. W. *The Stages of Economic Growth*. Cambridge: Cambridge University Press, 1960.

THREE

The Choices Before Us:

Alternative World Food Balances

To The Year 2000

Anthony S. Rojko

Mr. Rojko is program leader of the Commodities Area, Foreign Demand and Competition Division, Economic Research Service, of the U.S. Department of Agriculture. Having joined the Department in 1949, he is presently active in making projections of U.S. agricultural exports, foreign supply and demand, as well as trade in agricultural products by countries and regions. His duties require making long-range projections as well as short-term forecasts.

He has a Bachelor of Arts degree in agricultural economics from the University of Massachusetts and a Master of Arts degree in agricultural economics from the University of Connecticut. He has also done graduate work at the University of Chicago.

INTRODUCTION

The marked shift in the world food situation from surplus toward shortage and back again toward more adequate supplies over the last four to five years has generated much concern as to likely food balances in the future. Such speculation is not new; abundant supplies and low prices in the late 1960s and very early 1970s touched off fears of chronic surpluses and excess production capacity. Then, widespread production shortfalls in 1972 and 1974 touched off even greater concern over possible famine or widespread undernutrition in a world perpetually short of food (6, 7, 26, 27, 31). * Substantially larger harvests in 1975 and 1976 have eased some of these concerns and strengthen the contention that the world does have a capacity to feed itself (16, 34, 35, 37, 42, 43, 46).

Despite fundamental differences in their conclusions, both feast and famine theorists agree on the key factors common to surplus and shortage problems. Where supply is concerned, analysts agree on the importance of natural resource (generally measures defined roughly in terms of arable or potentially arable land and water supplies), and productivity (generally defined roughly as the know-how and inputs needed to augment natural resources in the production of food). In the case of demand, there is agreement on the importance of changes in population and income. A fifth factor, the policy context or institutional setting, is also agreed to be crucial (4, 15, 21, 29). But after identifying these key variables, many of the feast and famine theorists ignore the question of factor balance or the relationship between all five variables interacting simultaneously. In particular, short-term cyclical imbalances among these variables are often construed as indicators of long-term future prospects.

This paper reexamines the world food situation of the last several decades in general and the last four or five years in particular with special reference to the interaction of these two sets of variables—resource and productivity factors on the supply side and population and income factors on the demand side.† Special attention is given to the less-developed countries (LDCs) and to differences between the low-income and higher-income countries of the developing world.

The last section of this discussion projects grain production, consumption, trade levels, and growth rates—given alternative institu-

*Refer to Bibliographical Notes at the end of the chapter.

† The author wishes to acknowledge the help of Patrick O'Brien and Donald Regier in the preparation of the paper. The conclusions reached in this paper are not necessarily those of the U.S. Department of Agriculture.

The projections presented in this paper are part of a larger study involving Donald Regier, livestock; Arthur Coffing, oilseeds; Patrick O'Brien, grains; Robert Barry, rice; and Linda Bailey, statistical and computer support. Several people have helped develop the computer programs beginning with Francis Urban and Hilarius Fucho during the main development stage, followed by Fenton Sands and Martin Schwartz. Significant contributions were made by a number of other Economic Research Service analysts including Wade Gregory, John Link, Myles Mielke, John Parker, Leroy Quance, and Allan Smith.

tional setting—and resource productivity, population, and income mixes with special regard to the changing food situation in the LDCs.

The paper suggests that several outcomes are feasible and society's choice might prove either the feast or famine analyst to be correct. If the choices are wise, both the feast and famine analysts could be proven wrong. However, these choices must be made in the light of the food problems that have surfaced. They differ in the developed as well as the developing world but must be reconciled in a total world framework.

The concern in the developed countries is that of adjustment which leads to problems in at least three main areas: (1) The relationship of short-term production variability, pricing instability, and grain reserve policy, and their impact on long-term production; (2) The correct assessment of climatic change as it impacts on productivity; and (3) The potential impact of environmental constraints on production costs.

In contrast, problems in the developing world are those of distribution and economic development. These problems may be aggravated because of imbalances in rates of growth in income, population, and agricultural production. Under these circumstances, dependence on grain imports from the developed world could be expected to continue. An important consequence is continued malnutrition, and massive transfers of food aid are at best only temporary solutions. Furthermore, such aid may impede or postpone fundamental adjustments needed to generate the development process. The alternative projections for the developing world treat population, income, agricultural and nonagricultural productivity, and resource use as a bundle generating a balanced sustained growth in all sectors of the economy.

HISTORIC PERSPECTIVE AND LONG-RANGE POTENTIAL

Historical Trends

From the end of World War II until the early 1970s, both the developed and the developing countries made strong, steady gains in expanding with growth roughly equal in both the richer developed countries and the poorer developing countries as is evident in Figures 3.1, 3.2, and 3.3. World grain production—the single largest component of the world food supply—rose every year with the exception of 1961, 1963, and 1966, as shown in Fig. 3.4, when poor crops concen-

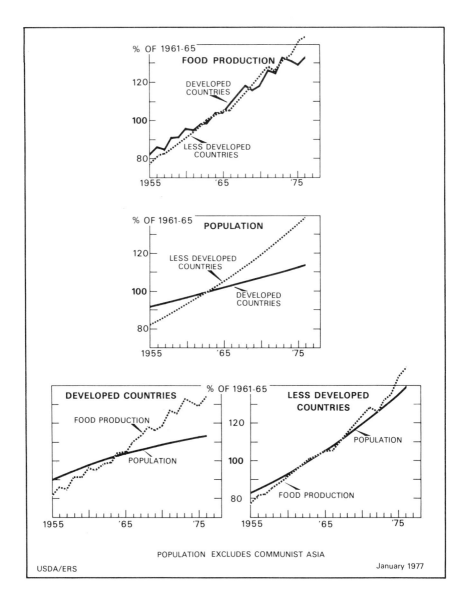

Fig. 3.1 Food Production and Population: Developed and Less Developed Countries

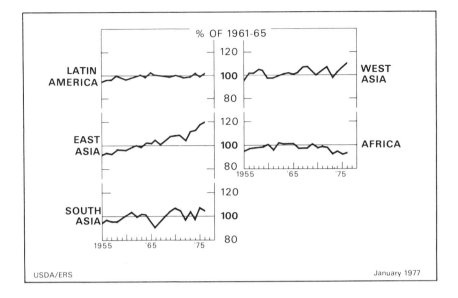

Fig. 3.2 Food Production Per Capita: Less Developed Countries

trated in either the Soviet Union or the Indian subcontinent offset generalized production increases in the rest of the world. This steady growth in food output occurred despite production controls in the developed exporting countries, particularly the United States, and despite the dampening effect of low-priced concessional imports on indigenous production in the developing countries. The low prices generated by abundant supplies made marked increases in food consumption in the developing countries and feed use of grain in the developed countries possible. Consumption increases, however, were skewed, with the developing countries, growth rate somewhat higher because of large imports of food from the developed countries, particularly toward the end of the period.

The population versus income and productivity versus resource balances generating these two and a half decades of growth differed from country to country, but more markedly between the developed and developing country aggregates. In the developed countries, productivity gains generated the bulk of the supply increase and income

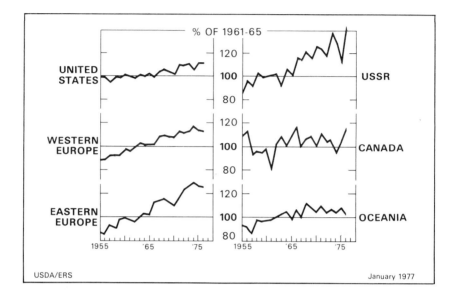

Fig. 3.3 Food Production Per Capita: Developed Countries

gains generated the bulk of the consumption increase as is illustrated by Figures 3.5, 3.6, and 3.7. Population—increasing less than 1.2 percent per year for the period as a whole—accounted for less than half of the developed countries' growth in demand. Increases in natural resources, primarily land committed to agricultural production, accounted for less than a fifth of the production gains. For example, area in grains in the developed countries actually stagnated with virtually no change in area harvested in 1969-71 as compared with 1948-52. In the United States alone, as much as 65 million acres of cropland were diverted from production under government programs in the 1960s.

Somewhat the reverse situation prevailed in the developing countries. Increases in population—averaging some 2.5 percent per year over the period as a whole—accounted for more than 85 percent of the increase in demand for grain. Over 60 percent of the increase in the developing countries' production was generated by expanding area,

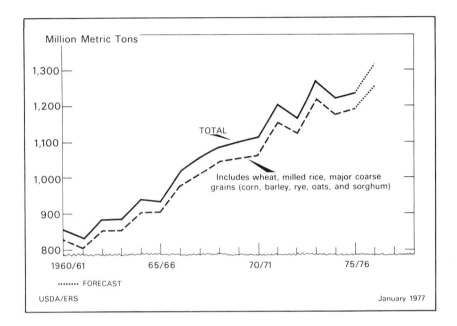

Fig. 3.4 World Grain Production

rather than gains in productivity.

The differences between population and income balances in the developed and developing countries translated into markedly different food situations. In both groups of countries, production in the early 1970s was more than 30 percent above the levels of the 1960s and more than 50 percent above the levels of the mid-1950s. On a per capita basis, however, food production in the developing countries increased less than .5 percent per year compared with 1.5 percent in the developed world. The developed countries' growing affluence—rather than population growth—generated a decided shift away from a grain-based diet toward higher livestock protein diets, often at the expense of large imports of grain for use as livestock feed from the United States, Canada, Australia, and Argentina. In the majority of the developing countries increasingly large transfers of food—primarily grain—from the developed countries became necessary to sustain per

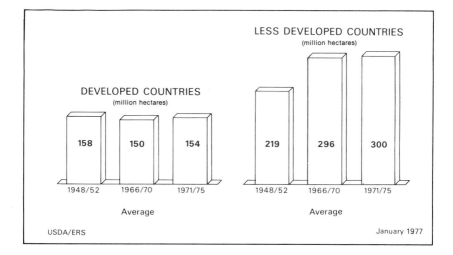

Fig. 3.5 Grain Area

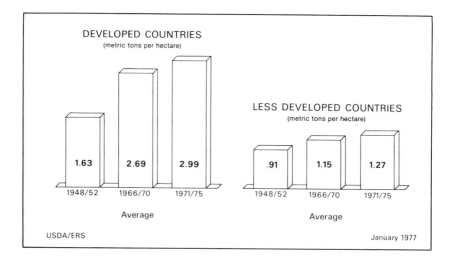

Fig. 3.6 Grain Yields

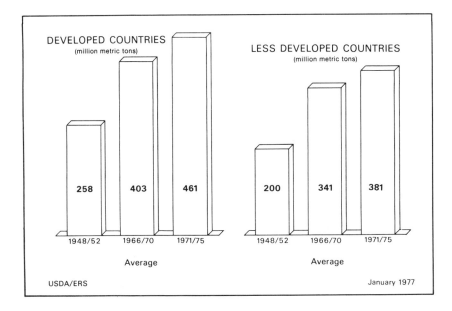

DEVELOPED COUNTRIES
(million metric tons)

LESS DEVELOPED COUNTRIES
(million metric tons)

| 258 | 403 | 461 | | 200 | 341 | 381 |

1948/52   1966/70   1971/75   1948/52   1966/70   1971/75

Average   Average

USDA/ERS   January 1977

Fig. 3.7 Total Grain Production

capita consumption growth of less than 1 percent per year in average production years and to avoid famine in shortfall years.

The different productivity versus resource balances also generated markedly different agricultural systems. Agriculture in the higher-income countries became flexible, energy and capital intensive and characterized by owner-operator mixed crop livestock systems. Its institutions in the affluent nations were designed to encourage farmers to take the risks inherent in large-scale capital investment and adoption of the latest agricultural technology. Further, the market orientation and high degree of product specialization encouraged trade among regions and across national boundaries. Both the physical and institutional bases of this type of agriculture have been reorganized a number of times to meet the changing food and fibers needs of expanding, but more importantly, increasingly affluent, populations.

Agriculture in the lower-income countries developed along more subsistence or semisubsistence lines (10). Institutions were structured to meet the initial needs of expanding agricultural production—i.e., expanding use of resources—but were generally unable to meet the needs of a sustained, resource- and productivity-balanced expansion. This traditional system was capable of a limited, piecemeal adoption of technological improvements borrowed from the developed countries. Purely technical change without institutional change, however, could not be sustained and left the bulk of the agricultural sector out of the development process. It should be kept in mind that, outstanding as the Green Revolution has been in aggregate terms in the lower-income countries, the biggest successes have been concentrated in the developed countries.

The net effects of these different factor balances and agricultural systems are clearly apparent in absolute per capita consumption levels. Disparities in the distribution of wealth and income growth have had an overwhelming impact on the distribution of food around the world. Over the period in question, the higher-income countries were able to make a decided shift toward indirect consumption of grain (i.e., as livestock feed), pushing total direct and indirect consumption to 800 kilograms per person in North America and in excess of 450 kilograms on average.

The low levels of income in developing countries are major explanations of why these countries with roughly 55 percent of the world's people consume daily about 40 percent of the world's caloric food energy supplies, mostly in the form of grain. In countries such as India, people consume less than 185 kilograms of grain per capita each year. The billion people in the rich nations, with tastes for livestock products, use practically as much cereal for livestock feed as the 2 billion people in the low-income nations use directly as food.

Recent Events

The short supplies and high food prices of 1972-75 stand out in marked contrast to the relatively abundant supplies and low prices of the preceeding two decades. Exceptionally marked and widespread variations in weather caused both drought and flooding in 1972 and 1974 and reduced world food production in absolute terms for the first time in more than two decades. Per capita production fell back to levels reached more than a decade earlier. World grain production in these two years fell over 100 million tons short of trend. The effect of these two years of shortfall on the world market and in turn on the major importing and exporting countries was magnified by a number of other, essentially exogenous, political and economic developments. Contrary to previous occasions, the Soviets and Chinese decided to translate their shortfalls directly into world import demand. The import demand of conventional purchasers in Western Europe and Japan also reached new highs as income growth peaked in an unusually large number of countries simultaneously.

Many of the inherent weaknesses of the institutional settings, as well as the population versus income, and resource versus productivity balances of the 1950s and 1960s, became apparent from 1972/73 through 1975/76, when developed-country feed demand and developing-country food demand bid against short supplies and pushed world grain prices up as much as 150 percent. In the developing world, a number of countries faced widespread shortages and drastic increases in the cost of food imports, which, in turn, led to significantly lower per capita consumption. The developed countries' livestock sectors—particularly in the major grain exporting countries—underwent drastic adjustments as grain available for feeding tightened and livestock-feed price ratios fell off to 15-20 year lows.

While many of the most pressing of these food problems eased in 1975/76 as world food production moved back to normal and actually exceeded trend in 1976/77, the basic questions raised remain valid. Chief among these are questions of the world's capacity to feed itself without reverting to institutionalized malnutrition in poor countries or massive transfers of food aid from the developed countries. Research by a number of physical scientists and technicians have provided measures of food production potential to answer questions of capacity (8, 12, 13, 14, 22, 30). Beyond the questions of capacity, which are addressed subsequently, are questions as to the implications of different institutional settings and their effect on alternative productivity versus resource and population versus income balances, particularly in the developing countries. These are addressed in the final projections section of this paper.

Food Production Potential

The short food supplies and high prices of the last four or five years have generated a new wave of Malthusian pessimism about future food balances. The writings of the Club of Rome (26, 27), Lester Brown (7), and others (8, 25) emphasize faltering growth in agricultural productivity, limited natural resources, and accelerating growth in population to support their general conclusions that the world is entering a period of more or less chronic shortages, high prices, and market rationing of food. A number of other agricultural economists and physical scientists (8, 22, 23, 34, 35, 45), on the other hand, have concluded that, given the world's current production potential, the food situation could well improve rather than deteriorate in the years to come.

Underlying the optimism of the physical scientists and many agricultural economists are the results of a number of recent studies. Analyses done as recently as 1971 by V. A. Kovda (22) and 1975 by P. H. Buringh et. al (8) confirm and extend the conclusions of earlier studies, including the 1967 *President's Science Advisory Committee Report* (45) and the FAO Indicative World Plan (17). At current levels of agricultural technology and scientific knowledge, the world's supply of potentially arable area is somewhat in excess of one and a half times the area currently under cultivation. Only about 41 percent of the land determined through extensive soil surveys and soil taxonomy studies to be arable is currently cultivated. Admittedly, there are a number of distributional problems. The largest reserves of potentially arable area are concentrated in tropical, and to a lesser extent, temperate areas of Latin America, Africa, and North America. Admittedly, land reserves are quite small in heavily populated Europe and most of Asia, and large Latin-American and African reserves are often quite far from population centers. Most of the world's uncultivated land is also already in use—either for forestry or range or some combination of the two. More intensive use of these reserves, even by assuming current standards as a maximum, and greater use of the world market, however, could ease existing as well as any foreseeable distribution problems.

Similar physical studies on the use and availability of water also point to large, unused potential. A recent study by Leith and Whittaker (23) which measures water resource potential in terms of biomass, points to upper limits of 4,000 grams per square meter $(2/m^2)$ with averages in the range of 650 $2/m^2$. For purposes of comparison, rice yields in land-tight Asia are reported under 200 $2/m^2$ or less than one-third of average. Substantial gains in food and overall agricultural production are to be made without the large investments needed to reach Leith and Whittaker's average through more immediate improvements in water management practices, expanded investment in irrigation facilities, and adaptation of crop systems designed to optimize the productivity of existing natural water supplies.

Studies analyzing the production implications of existing yet un-adopted agricultural technology point to potentially large gains as well. Even if the average grain yields of the developed countries are substituted for the appreciably higher technologically feasible yields generally used in measures of potential, the gains to be made in the LDCs through productivity improvements are still in the order of 400 to 500 percent. Realizing any significant portion of these potential productivity increases, however, will depend on more effective transfer of technology to the LDCs and to the small farmers of the LDCs, in particular. While there is no absolute guarantee that technology developed in the high-income temperate zone will be applicable in the lower-income tropical zone countries, expanded use of soil taxonomy techniques similar to those outlined in recent Soil Conservation Service materials (40) can facilitate more effective transfers than in the past.

Combining the arable area, water supply, and technology conclusions of these recent studies points to food production potentials in excess of foreseeable demand well beyond 2000. The Buringh study referred to above computed the absolute maximum food production capacity of the world at almost 40 times present production levels, assuming full use of all soil and water resources and assuming full use of modern production technology. Estimates by Chou, Harmon, and Esbenshade of the Hudson Institute point to a range of food production possibilities up to ten times current levels (10). Other studies, including those of Leith and Whittaker (23), DeWit (14), and Kovda (22), point to roughly comparable potentials. Some may judge these figures unrealistically high, particularly in view of the implicit assumption that all inputs—fertilizers, seeds, improved varieties, pesticides, and machinery—would be available at the necessary time and in adequate amounts needed. Nevertheless, the conclusion stands that there are adequate soil and water resources, and sufficient existing technology to greatly increase food production. The potential appears to be such that for a long time to come the availability of other inputs, institutional or organization problems, or crucial resource, productivity, population, and income imbalances are likely to constrain production increases. Substantial improvement in the world food situation is not likely to be easy or instantaneous, as the following projections alternatives indicate; however, they are possible.

Food Demand Potential

Food availability, population growth, affluency, and particularly income distribution will continue to be the main determinants of growth in food demand to 2000 and beyond. Only in recent years has the problem of malnutrition, or unmet food demand, been viewed as a problem of development—not as a consequence of, but rather as a major factor contributing to underdevelopment. Thus, growing concern can be expected regarding the relationship of poverty and the productivity of human capital as it impinges on development and food demand potential.

The shift toward more varied diets, particularly the increase in the per capita consumption of meat and livestock products, will undoubtedly continue with growth in income. It is also quite likely that some small increases in meat consumption levels in North America would result from better distribution of income, particularly if special food and other programs that directly or indirectly benefit low-income people are continued and if the real number of people at the poverty level is reduced (32). Most likely the countries of Western Europe will not raise per capita meat comsumption or feed usage to North American levels. Consumption patterns in countries like Japan may continue to be Westernized, but probably not to the extent expected earlier as consumers learn more about the health effects of food products produced in high-energy, chemical-intensive settings or through the use of additives. Similar developments are likely in the lower-income developed countries, where per capita meat consumption is still well below levels in the higher-income countries.

In contrast, only limited improvements in an essentially cereal-based diet are expected in many of the developing countries; income growth is not likely to be strong enough to generate more than a small shift toward an animal protein diet. Millions of people in these countries are currently inadequately fed. FAO estimated that the food intake of over 400 million people of the lower-income countries does not meet the "maintenance cost of energy," (42, pp. 65-67). As many as 30 percent of the population in some areas are subject to food deficiencies.

Reutlinger and Selowsky (37) in a recent study also estimated developing world calorie deficits in a range of 350-488 thousand million in the mid-1960s or about one-third higher than estimates obtained through use of national average per capita caloric data. A 400 thousand million calorie deficit a day is equivalent to about 38 million metric tons of food grain annually—about 4 percent of current world production. Reutlinger and Selowsky project calorie deficits to 1985 and 1990 and conclude that the total calorie deficit would remain virtually unchanged by 1990 if income distributions remain the same. They also conclude that, without marked income redistribution, it would take rates of growth well above those currently forecast to achieve per capita consumption levels sufficient to eliminate calorie deficits in the lowest-income classes. Elimination of nutritional deficits under such circumstances would also quite likely require a rate of growth in food production and consumption that could be achieved only if large subsidies were paid to maintain high incentive prices to farmers and low food prices to consumers. A realistic solution to the problem therefore must lie in programs directed toward target groups specifically designed to allow people of low income to achieve minimal standards of nutrition.

Diets may vary widely in terms of varieties of food consumed but yet provide adequate nutrients. For example, expert observation of the People's Republic of China suggests that the Chinese population is receiving adequate nutrition and that few, if any, suffer from malnutrition or undernutrition (38). Per capita cereal consumption in China is about 500 pounds (227 kg.); yet there are limited, if any, nutritional problems. In comparison, many other countries have *average* per capita consumption considerably higher, but yet substantial parts of their population experience malnutrition and undernourishment because of uneven distribution. The egalitarian approach of the Chinese to income distribution and food consumption minimizes the possibility of individuals using income and wealth to finance the conversion of grain into livestock products. This situation contrasts sharply with the relationship among income, wealth, and nutrition found in most other countries.

ALTERNATIVE FUTURES

Following is a quantitative evaluation of the effects of several alternative sets of assumptions on grain production and consumption growth rates in the developing countries and the production and trade adjustments implied for the developed countries.[1] Treatment of the centrally planned economies—the USSR, Eastern Europe, and the People's Republic of China—is limited to projections of the imports and exports necessary to balance trade on the world level.

ASSUMPTIONS

Two basic sets of assumptions about future world cereals production, consumption, and trade are projected: (1) a developing world in which production and consumption growth rates result in only limited improvement in the world food situation, and, in contrast, (2) a developing world in which sustained action is taken to improve the food situation substantially, but still within the limits of the achievable. The two basic sets are considered to have similar probabilities of success with the outcome depending on the policies adopted. Each bundle of assumptions reflects different possibilities for key economic and policy variables. Other alternatives are presented which further study the implications of modifying policy constraints. A mathematical model is used to project the impact of the different alternative assumptions.

Projections of food supply and demand to 2000 are subject to a number of qualifications. Estimating rates of change in population, income, and a number of other crucial supply variables, as well as their interrelationships for more than ten or fifteen years, calls for individual projection studies. The whole complex of income growth, population growth, resource endowment, technical growth in food production, and growth in industrial production is closely interrelated. *Rapid population growth increases demand for fixed resources and can easily affect productivity adversely,* given the scarcity of natural resources and capital relative to labor generally found in the developing countries. Increasing labor productivity and employment, on the other hand, seems to be necessary if the per capita income levels generally associated with

Table 3.1   Population, Income, Productivity, and Resource Growth Rates to 2000

Country/Region	Population	Income	Productivity	Resource
	Compound Annual Growth Rate [1] (% per year)			
1970 Base				
Developed Countries	1.0	3.6	2.4	.2
Exporters[2]	1.3	2.3	2.2	.4
Importers[3]	.8	4.9	2.9	−.2
Developing Countries	2.5	2.0	1.6	1.0
Exporters[4]	2.5	2.3	1.4	2.0
Importers	2.5	2.0	1.6	1.0
Latin America	2.9	2.9	1.2	2.6
Developing Africa and West Asia	2.6	2.1	1.1	.8
Other Developing Asia	2.4	1.0	1.8	.7
Alternative I				
Developed Countries	.7	2.6	1.3	.7
Exporters[2]	1.0	2.1	1.2	1.0
Importers[3]	.6	3.0	1.5	.1
Developing Countries	2.6	3.2	1.8	1.0
Exporters[4]	2.5	2.4	1.2	1.5
Importers	2.6	3.2	1.9	.9
Latin America	2.8	3.6	1.7	1.4
Developing Africa and West Asia	2.9	3.6	2.2	.5
Other Developing Asia	2.4	2.3	1.8	.9
Alternative II				
Developed Countries	.7	2.6	1.4	.4
Exporters[2]	1.0	2.1	1.3	.5
Importers[3]	.6	3.0	1.5	.1
Developing Countries	2.3	3.4	2.2	1.0
Exporters[4]	2.2	2.7	1.5	1.2
Importers	2.3	3.5	2.2	.9
Latin America	2.5	3.8	2.1	1.4
Developing Africa and West Asia	2.6	3.9	2.5	.5
Other Developing Asia	2.2	2.4	2.2	.9

SOURCE: USDA/Economics, Statistics, and Cooperatives Service.

[1]   Growth rates under 1970 base are historical rates based on the period 1960-75 except for income computed from 1960 to 1970. Growth rates for 2000 computed from base 1970.   [2]   United States, Canada, South Africa, Oceania.   [3]   Western Europe, Japan.   [4]   Argentina, Thailand.

slowed population growth rates are to be reached. *International comparisons among nations show that birth rates and income growth tend to be inversely related.* The same tendency is also likely to be true within nations. Thus, broad participation in accelerated income growth seems to be essential if any slowing of population growth is to be achieved in the developing countries. Given current per capita consumption levels in these countries, income growth means increased food demand which, given relatively fixed agricultural resources, must be met largely through technological advances in agriculture. The scenarios outlined below consider these population, income, and productivity interrelationships in the light of alternative policy assumptions. The combinations of population, income, and productivity growth rates used in Alternatives I and II in Table 3.1 reflect the kind of growth expected from general tendencies in the past, providing similar developmental policies and constraints are followed. In contrast, the several other alternatives analyzed evaluate the impact that more drastic policies or lack of policies would have on future production and consumption growth rates.

ALTERNATIVES

Alternative I

Alternative I postulates a modified continuation of the trends of the 1950s, 1960s, and early 1970s. No marked breakthroughs are assumed in slowing population growth, in substantially raising nutrition levels, in augmenting limited physical resources, in reforming agrarian institutions, or in accelerating technological change. The specific assumptions are as follows:

Population. The U.N.'s modified median growth rates used in Alternative I provide for little slowing in population growth rates in the key food-short LDCs. Some limited tapering off in growth rates occurs in the 1990s, but only after sustained high growth through the 1980s. The compound annual growth rate for the LDCs as a whole is projected at 2.7 percent from 1970 to 1985, and estimated to be about 2.5 percent from 1985 to 2000, for a thirty-year rate of 2.6 percent. These growth rates translate into an annual increment of 86 million people in 2000, compared with 1975's increment of 50 million people.

In both cases, roughly three-fifths of this increase is concentrated in already overpopulated, food-deficit developing Asia. The compound rate for the developed countries over the same thirty-year period is 0.7 percent, which pulls the world growth down to 1.9 percent.

Income Growth. Compound annual growth rates for per capita income are assumed to be 2.9 percent for the developed countries and 2.3 percent for the less developed countries. This level of income growth for the LDCs pushes per capita levels from $436 in 1975 to $900 in 2000 in terms of 1975 purchasing power. While economic theory holds that with higher real incomes, consumer demand for cereals drops and demand for livestock products increases, the 2000 levels projected for the LDCs are not high enough to generate much movement out of cereals. On the contrary, these higher income levels are likely to generate increased demand for cereals in many areas as consumers reduce intake of lower preference starchy crops and pulses. The wealthier countries of East Asia and the OPEC, as well as a few grain exporters, however, are likely to undergo appreciably larger shifts from cereals to livestock products. In these selected LDCs and in the developed countries in general, decreases in consumer demand for cereals and increases in demand for livestock products are small at low-income levels, then rise significantly at intermediate levels, and ultimately taper off at very high levels. At the high-income levels of the most developed countries, both income growth and consumer response are projected to drop off because of their high levels of affluence.

Technology and Production Policies. Under Alternative I, the LDCs are assumed to make only limited progress in revamping agriculture to meet their changing food and fiber needs. While considerable effort may be expected to reform agrarian institutions and to accelerate technological modernization, it is assumed that only modest success occurs by 2000.

In the area of *institutional reform* in the developing countries, the expense of reforming land tenure arrangements is likely to be prohibitive enough and the effects disruptive enough in the short term to justify government inaction, despite unquestionable long-term benefits. The situation could lead to agricultural sections characterized by a small group of large, commercial, progressive farms and a large group of small, subsistence farms.

Unresolved problems in product and input marketing are also likely to be aggravated by large populations and increased need for resource-augmenting nonfarm inputs. Increases in urban populations—often underemployed and unemployed and virtually always poor—are likely to strain product marketing systems and lead to subsidized food and lower supply procurement prices. The consequently higher import requirements projected under this scenario would most likely dry up much of the foreign exchange needed to import high productivity inputs or the machinery and technology needed to expand production facilities at home. The short supply and high price of inputs and generally low procurement prices would discourage indigenous production and dampen the average LDCs farmer's incentive to make the long-term investments and development planning necessary to modernize agriculture.

Funds available for the indigenous research, extension, and education necessary to develop and disseminate a specifically tropical or semitropical agricultural technology are likely to be limited; most LDCs will continue to import agricultural technology poorly suited to their own particular problems. Critical technological breakthroughs needed to raise productivity despite unresolved land tenure and marketing problems are consequently unlikely to be forthcoming.

Adoption of updated agricultural technology and use of *high productivity inputs* in the LDCs are assumed under Alternative I to grow at a rate approximating the trends of the last twenty years. Productivity increase is projected at 1.8 percent per year while resource use grows at 1 percent under Alternative I.

Raising productivity in the LDCs will continue to depend largely on injections of improved inputs—i.e., chemical fertilizers, pesticides, high-yielding varieties, et cetera—as well as updated technology—i.e., water control, multiple-cropping, selective mechanization, and so on. Without these energy injections, the developing countries will be unable to replace closed, farming systems yielding little more than a subsistence return with open, energy-intensive systems yielding appreciably higher returns.

While the assumptions outlined above apply to most of the LDCs, there are exceptions. Both South Korea and Taiwan are assumed to follow the Japanese agricultural development example. Use of energy-related inputs is assumed to increase at a faster rate in the OPEC countries and in particular in Indonesia.

Input usage patterns are not assumed to change markedly in the developed countries. While considerable effort is being expanded in many of the more advanced countries to develop alternative sources, it is generally assumed that fossil-based fuels will continue to be the major source of energy used in agriculture to 2000. A number of adjustments, such as adoption of energy-conserving practices, including minimum tillage, is expected. Agriculture in the developed world is projected to continue being both capital-intensive and energy-intensive. A particular country's degree of capital and energy intensity will vary according to its resource endowment, factor availabilities, and grain-livestock mix. The tendency in the United States toward larger units, replacement of labor with machinery, rapid increases in purchased inputs, and product specialization, with increases in output per man hour as well as per hectare, is expected to predominate elsewhere, particularly in the major exporting countries and the larger countries of Western Europe. Some variation is expected in a few of the Western European countries and particularly in Japan. In the Japanese case, farms are expected to remain small. Increases in productivity are likely to result from the further substitution of smaller scaled, two-wheel tractor type of technology for the draft animal and the farm laborer and from continued emphasis on fertilizer, pesticides, and high-yielding varieties. The increasing energy and capital intensity of both the U.S. and the Japanese systems, however, is expected to put a premium on efficient use of high-cost, skilled labor.

Alternative II

Alternative II traces out the effects of slowed population growth, higher incomes, and better organization of agriculture in the less developed countries. The assumptions regarding the developed countries are essentially the same as under Alternative I. Changes in production, consumption, and trade in the higher-income countries are generated in response to changes in supply and demand in the LDCs and their effect on the world market.

Population. Under Alternative II, population growth in the LDCs is assumed to slow appreciably. Growth from 1970 to 1985 is assumed to average somewhat lower than the 2.7 percent of Alternative I, particularly in the early 1980s. Further slowdowns through the mid-1980s and 1990s, however, are expected to pull the growth rate for the period as a whole down to 2.3 percent. The annual increment in 2000 would be 65 million people, compared with a 86 million increment under the higher Alternative I growth rate.

Income growth. Per capita income growth is assumed to increase appreciably faster under Alternative II because of progress in slowing population growth, raising labor productivity in goods and service sectors outside agriculture, and—at least in part—in substantially larger capital and technical aid flows from the developed countries. A large part of any increase in income, however, will still have to be generated in agriculture and related sectors, given what is expected to be the essentially agrarian nature of the average LDC economy. Per capita income under this alternative would rise at an annual average rate of close to 2.7 percent compared with 2.3 under Alternative I. Some shifts from essentially cereal diets to mixed cereal-livestock diets would be expected; this shift in demand could lead to accelerated development or expansion of grain-feeding operations. These increases in grainfeeding would be mostly in parts of East Asia, North Africa/Middle East, and Latin America. Shifts would still be minimal at most, however, in sub-Sahara developing Africa, South Asia, and parts of East Asia.

Technology and Production Policies. Under Alternative II, the less developed countries are assumed to have made significant progress in reorganizing agriculture so as to raise agricultural productivity levels. These increases in productivity are due as much to institutional and organizational changes as to expanded use of improved inputs to augment limited resource bases.

In the area of institutional reform, the LDCs are assumed to have resolved some of the issues of resource tenure—i.e., the use and/or ownership of the major factors of production—in such a way as to encourage long-range investment and development planning. Sufficient public and private credit is assumed to be available to make capital expansion and use of high-cost inputs possible for the small- and medium-size farm as well as the larger agribusiness.

Improvements in input and product market systems are assumed to have eased key distribution bottlenecks and to have made more efficient movement of larger food supplies in both urban and rural areas possible. Government food subsidy expenditures are expected to be lower than under Alternative I, not only because of lower population levels, but also because of technological innovations reducing product costs and increased income growth—more equitably distributed—reducing the plight of the urban poor. The technological innovations necessary to improve agricultural productivity and lower production costs while keeping farm returns high are assumed to be the direct result of investments in primary research on specific LDC problems—possibly conducted at the international level—and secondary education and extension work at the national and local level.

IMPLICATIONS

It is generally agreed that it is possible to make projections for the next decade based on reasonably certain assumptions. Projections to the year 2000, however, are based on assumptions which are themselves projections. Attaching probabilities upon projections to 2000 is consequently difficult at best, particularly because projection exercises are designed to test alternatives and, it is hoped, influence policy changes to avoid potential supply and demand problems.

For the developed world as a whole, the projections indicate that the capital and energy intensive, market-and trade-oriented agricultural systems currently in place will be able to meet growing domestic food and feed demand. Given the productive capacities of most of the deficit, high-income countries, continuation of present agricultural and trade policies would keep self-sufficiency levels in most of Western Europe at about current levels. Countries like Japan, of course, will continue to import the bulk of their nonrice grain consumption. The developed exporters—the United States, Canada, and Australia—appear to have the physical capacity to expand production to meet any of the world import demand levels projected under Alternatives I and II, assuming good weather.

Under Alternative I, the higher world import demand situation, grain area in the developed regions expands at a rate of .7 percent per year as seen in Table 3.1. However, under Alternative II the growth rate is reduced to .4 percent per year as increased productivity and a better balance between population, income, and productivity in the

LDCs reduces their grain imports. The grain area harvested in the major exporting countries under Alternative I is about 43 percent of total arable area, compared with 33 percent in 1970 and the previous record of about 45 percent in the early 1950s. Under Alternative II, the percentage drops to 38 percent. However, the area devoted to soybeans was only a small portion of total arable area in the early 1950s and since then the proportion has increased rapidly; it is projected to continue rising through the year 2000. A considerable part of the increase in soybean area is on land formerly in corn production thus indicating a much tighter resource constraint than is evident from the above comparisons. Total grain area in the world under Alternative I would account for about 52 percent of the arable area, as compared with 48 percent in 1970. If total arable area expands at the rate of the last two decades, grain area in 2000 would account for about the same share of both the exporters and the world's arable area as in 1973/74.

In contrast, productivity in the developed countries is projected to increase at an annual rate of 1.3 percent under Alternative I and 1.4 percent under Alternative II. The slightly higher rate under Alternative II reflects the use of a smaller but more efficient resource base. Yield increases under the two alternatives range from 40 to 50 percent higher than in the base 1970 period in most of the developed countries. Yields, however, are well within the bounds of existing technology and are based on an assumption of average weather.

Continued high energy costs in the developed countries could mean inflationary pressure on agriculture as a basic materials industry. It also appears that agriculture would not fare as well under high rates of inflation as under low rates. In general, problems of pricing, chronic shortages or surpluses—either from natural disasters including weather or from policy decisions—will continue to be the main problems in the developed countries as their agricultural sectors adjust to changing foreign demand and competition.

Because agriculture is a small sector of the aggregate economy in the developed world, cost and efficiency factors are the prime movers of the mix in the resource bundle. In contrast, agriculture is still the dominant sector in most LDCs; thus, resource use and agricultural production is more closely interrelated with population growth, income growth, and growth in the nonagricultural sector. The increase in the resource base at an annual rate of 1.5-2.0 percent in the LDCs was larger than the increase in productivity at 1.0-1.5 percent during 1950-65. The projected period calls for a reversal of the roles of productivity and resource use. Area is projected to grow at an annual rate of about 1 percent under Alternative I and remains essentially the same for Alternative II. The expansion of area is limited, particularly in those parts of Asia where the people-land ratio is relatively high. Most of the area expansion in these countries would be from double-cropping. On the other hand, in countries like Brazil, new lands could be brought into production.

Given the projected resource base, productivity in the developing countries is expected to increase at 1.8 percent per year under Alternative II. Both rates of increase are well within technological capabilities, as productivity in the LDCs is still relatively low compared to that in the developed world.

ALTERNATIVES

Specific implications and assumptions follow for both alternatives.

Alternative I

Under Alternative I, the cereal import gap of the LDCs could easily increase to 108 million metric tons by the year 2000, a level that is above current levels of 35 million tons and the 1970 level of 18 million tons as shown in Table 3.2. As a share of total usage, the gap would increase from 7 percent in 1970 to 14 percent by the year 2000. While the increase in percentage points may be small, the 108-million-ton figure would put a severe strain on the LDCs' generally weak foreign exchange position and could require large concessional sales or direct food aid from the developed countries.

Under Alternative I, the failure to do much to reduce population growth rates or raise agricultural productivity levels significantly limits grain production increase in LDCs to 2.8 percent per year. Thus, indigenous production barely exceeds the growth in population as evidenced by Table 3.3. As a result, the LDCs of most of Asia and Africa continue as essentially cereal-based economies. In Latin America, where the man-to-land ratio is much lower, livestock will continue to be an important source of calories. However, population

Table 3.2   Projected Grain Net Export to 2000

Country/Region	1970 Base	Alternative I	Alternative II
	(million metric tons)		
Developed Countries	32	134	78
Exporters[1]	68	202	151
Importers[2]	−36	−68	−74
Developing Countries	−18	−108	−51
Exporters[3]	11	32	32
Importers	−29	−140	−83
Latin America	−5	−30	−13
Developing Africa and West Asia	−10	−51	−31
Other Developing Asia	−14	−59	−39

SOURCE: USDA/Economics, Statistics, and Cooperatives Service

[1] United States, Canada, South Africa, Oceania.
[2] Western Europe, Japan.
[3] Argentina, Thailand.

pressure and infrastructure constraints are expected to preclude substantial improvements in diets in most of these countries as illustrated by Table 3.4. Consequently, improvements in per capita cereal and per capita food consumption are severely limited. Under Alternative I per capita cereal consumption increases from 173 kilos in 1970 to 199 in the year 2000, or at a rate of about .5 percent per year as demonstrated by Table 3.5.

The demand levels projected under Alternative I are well within the world's productive potential largely because of the capacity of the major exporting countries. However, periodic weather variations in a chronically grain-short developing world and policy fluctuations in the exporting countries aimed at accumulating or drawing down stocks could introduce an element of world supply and price instability. This aspect is pursued later.

Alternative II

Under Alternative II, the interaction of lower-population growth rates, higher-income growth rates, and agricultural reorganization

Table 3.3 Projected Grain Production to 2000

Country/Region	1970 Base	Alternative I	Alternative II
	(million metric tons)		
Developed Countries	402	729	675
Exporters[1]	267	514	464
Importers[2]	134	215	211
Developing Countries	279	639	690
Exporters[3]	30	68	66
Importers	249	571	624
Latin America	45	114	123
Developing Africa and West Asia	52	116	125
Other Developing Asia	152	341	376
	Compound Annual Growth Rate[4]		
	(% per year)		
Developed Countries	2.6	2.0	1.8
Exporters[1]	2.6	2.2	1.9
Importers[2]	2.6	1.6	1.5
Developing Countries	2.6	2.8	3.1
Exporters[3]	3.3	2.7	2.7
Importers	2.6	2.8	3.1
Latin America	3.8	3.1	3.4
Developing Africa and West Asia	1.9	2.7	3.0
Other Developing Asia	2.5	2.7	3.1

SOURCE: USDA/Economics, Statistics, and Cooperatives Service

[1] United States, Canada, South Africa, Oceania.
[2] Western Europe, Japan.
[3] Argentina, Thailand.
[4] Growth rates under 1970 base are historical rates based on the period 1960-75. Growth rates for 2000 are computed from base 1970.

generates substantial improvements in the LDCs' food balance. Cereal consumption levels are projected at 213 kilograms per capita, reflecting an average compound annual increase of about 0.7 percent. Net imports would fall off to 51 million metric tons. If Thailand and Argentina's net exports are broken out, however, even under Alternative II the LDCs' net imports would be 83 million metric tons, compared with 140 million tons under Alternative I. A substantially larger portion of this, however, would be imported for feed by the more af-

Table 3.4   Projected Grain Consumption to 2000

Country/Region	1970 Base	Alternative I	Alternative II
	(million metric tons)		
Developed Countries	374	594	598
Exporters[1]	202	312	313
Importers[2]	172	283	285
Developing Countries	300	747	740
Exporters[3]	18	36	34
Importers	281	711	707
Latin America	50	143	136
Developing Africa and West Asia	64	168	156
Other Developing Asia	167	400	415
	Compound Annual Growth Rate[4]		
	(% per year)		
Developed Countries	2.0	1.6	1.6
Exporters[1]	1.7	1.5	1.5
Importers[2]	2.4	1.7	1.7
Developing Countries	2.9	3.1	3.1
Exporters[3]	3.6	2.4	2.1
Importers	2.9	3.1	3.1
Latin America	4.3	3.6	3.4
Developing Africa and West Asia	2.6	3.3	3.0
Other Developing Asia	2.7	3.0	3.1

SOURCE: USDA/Economics, Statistics, and Cooperatives Service

[1] United States, Canada, South Africa, Oceania.
[2] Western Europe, Japan.
[3] Argentina, Thailand.
[4] Growth rates under 1970 base are historical rates based on the period 1960-75. Growth rates for 2000 are computed from base 1970.

fluent LDCs. Domestic production is projected to account for about 88 percent of the higher per capita consumption level because of sustained growth in production at an average rate of 3.1 percent per year as seen in Table 3.6. While imports increase in absolute numbers, the self-sufficiency ratio holds to 1970 levels. Under Alternative I, this ratio drops to 80 percent. The increases in grain availabilities projected under Alternative II are large enough and demand for livestock

Table 3.5   Projected Per Capita Grain Production and Consumption to 2000

COUNTRY/REGION	1970 BASE (kilograms)		ALTERNATIVE I (kilograms)		ALTERNATIVE II (kilograms)	
	PRODUCTION	CONSUMPTION	PRODUCTION	CONSUMPTION	PRODUCTION	CONSUMPTION
Developing Countries	160.7	172.7	169.9	198.6	198.2	212.6
Exporters[1]	489.2	293.5	526.0	278.5	555.7	286.3
Importers	148.6	167.7	157.2	195.8	185.6	210.3
Latin America	182.6	202.9	202.3	253.8	237.0	262.1
Developing Africa and West Asia	124.8	153.7	117.8	170.6	138.3	172.5
Other Developing Asia	150.1	165.0	163.7	192.0	193.9	214.0

	Compound Annual Growth Rates[2] (% per year)					
	PRODUCTION	CONSUMPTION	PRODUCTION	CONSUMPTION	PRODUCTION	CONSUMPTION
Developing Countries	.2	.5	.2	.5	.7	.7
Exporters[1]	.9	1.1	.2	-.2	.4	-.1
Importers	.1	.4	.2	.5	.7	.8
Latin America	1.0	1.4	.3	.7	.9	.9
Developing Africa and West Asia	-.6	.1	-.2	.3	.3	.3
Other Developing Asia	.2	.3	.3	.5	.9	.9

SOURCE: USDA/Economics, Statistics, and Cooperatives Service

[1]Argentina, Thailand.
[2]Growth rates under 1970 base are historical rates based on the period 1960-75. Growth rates for 2000 are computed from base 1970.

products buoyant enough to generate some growth in livestock feeding, particularly in dairy, pork, and poultry. While grains are projected to continue to make up the bulk of the LDC diet, livestock products will be an important source of calories, particularly in the OPEC countries, the high-income East Asian countries, the traditional livestock exporters of Latin America, and in parts of East Africa.

Effect of Income on Potential Food Demand

As indicated earlier, affluency and income distribution will continue to be the main determinants of growth in food demand to the year 2000. This section uses the following model to test the impact with and without price effects.

The model suggests that for each 10 percent rise in the income growth rate above the growth rate assumed in Alternative I, per capita consumption of grain would be expected to be 4 kilos higher in the year 2000 than levels projected under Alternative I. Thus, if the income growth rate postulated under Alternative I is changed from 2.3

Table 3.6   Projected Grain Self-Sufficiency Levels to 2000

Country/Region	1970 Base	Alternative I	Alternative II
		(%)	
Developed Countries	1.07	1.23	1.13
Exporters[1]	1.32	1.65	1.48
Importers[2]	.78	.76	.74
Developing Countries	.93	.86	.93
Exporters[3]	1.67	1.89	1.94
Importers	.89	.80	.88
Latin America	.90	.80	.90
Developing Africa and West Asia	.81	.69	.80
Other Developing Asia	.91	.85	.91

SOURCE: USDA/Economics, Statistics, and Cooperatives Service

Note: Grain self-sufficiency calculated as production divided by consumption.
[1]   United States, Canada, South Africa, Oceania.
[2]   Western Europe, Japan.
[3]   Argentina, Thailand.

to 3.3 percent, or roughly ending with income levels in the year 2000 about a third higher than they would be under Alternative I, per capita consumption levels are roughly 20 kilos higher than the Alternative I level of 202 kilos. If no compensating increases in production occur, the LDC grain import gap would increase by 70 million metric tons. This parametric assumed no price effect would occur. However, increase in income would increase price levels and reduce the increase in consumption somewhat. Under these circumstances, per capita consumption would increase by 14 kilos above Alternative I levels in the year 2000, and the increase in the trade gap would be reduced to 35 million metric tons.

In a recent study, Lyle Schertz tested the impact of what would happen if the income levels of Latin America prevailed in the rest of the developing world (38). It was assumed that by raising income to these levels, the LDC population below nutritional requirements would be reduced to approximately 13 percent, compared with a current estimate of 25 percent. Using 1970 as the impact year, raising income increased per capita consumption by 173 kilos. Holding other factors such as production and prices, the additional consumption would increase the trade gap by as much as 258 million metric tons.

On the other hand, if the Reutlinger criteria cited earlier in the paper were extended to the year 2000 in the framework of the Grain-Oilseeds-Livestocks model, GOL (see footnote 1), the trade gap associated with targeted distributions would require an additional 90 million metric tons compared to Reutlinger's equivalent of 38 million metric tons in the year 1965. These examples cited suggest that very substantial increases in income would have to occur in the developing countries before any significant progress is made to reduce the malnutrition problem. Thus, the solution to nutritional problems may require programs directed towards target groups—programs which are specifically designed to help people of low income achieve minimal standards of nutrition.

Impact of Climate on Grain Projections

The 1975 drought in the Soviet Union, the 1976 drought in Western Europe, and the recent weather problems in the United States have reactivated concern about the possibility of a changing world climate and its implications for future world food production, particularly lower grain yields (18, 20, 25, 33, 37, 39, 41). The impact of long-run changes in climate on yields would reflect a number of weather attributes—temperature, including levels and both seasonal and diurnal distribution effects, insolation, and moisture of both air and soil, including level and distribution.

In the recent controversy over climatic change, a number of theories have been advanced as to why the world's climate is expected to change. One theory is that a cooling trend in climate is occurring and that the trend will continue. Another is that a warming trend is likely in the future because of the increase in carbon dioxide (CO_2) in the air resulting from the burning of fossil fuels. A third theory suggests that there is a relationship between sunspot cycles and precipitation.

With respect to the cooling hypothesis, annual temperature data for the Northern Hemisphere shows a distinct rising trend from the 1880s to the 1940s, with a subsequent decrease to the 1970s. There is disagreement, however, as to whether this cooling trend is continuing. A continued cooling trend could have a serious negative impact on the northernmost agricultural areas of the United States and on agricultural areas in Canada and the USSR. The effect on production in the United States would be marginal, however, because there would be U.S. areas that might gain from a cooling trend.

As for the warming hypothesis, it is argued that the so-called "greenhouse effect" caused by emission of carbon dioxide is offsetting the cooling trend of recent decades. There has been speculation that the net effect of this warming would be a sharp decline in the productivity of much of the world's food-producing regions. But so far, no consensus has been reached.

With respect to sunspots, theorists suggest that a reoccurrence of a 1930s type of drought is "due" in the High Plains of the western United States in the mid-1970s. On a world basis, most drought conditions appear to occur at random, but the time and location on the U.S. High Plains appear to be an exception. Here, drought conditions have shown a marked regularity every twenty to twenty-five years corresponding to sunspot cycles.

Several conferences have been held on the relationship between climatic change and food production. At a December 1974 conference at Sterling Forest (41), there was general agreement that the 1955-71 period represented a sequence of favorable growing seasons, particularly for the United States. The June 1975 conference in Bellagio, Italy, noted that while the sharpest increases in corn yields in the United States occurred after 1960 when nitrogen fertilizer became cheap and plentiful, the U.S. Corn Belt had unusually favorable weather from 1956 through 1973 (25). The November 1975 conference in Toronto on "Living with Climatic Change" noted that "the remarkably consistent high productivity of North American agriculture from the mid-1950s to the early 1970s has been due to a combination of improved technology and exceptionally favorable weather . . . ." It was argued that this unusual run of good years has given a false impression of stability and security, and that the climate of the preceding century was much more variable and was characterized by periods of either sustained drought or moisture excess (39).

By modifying assumptions concerning future growth in grain yields, the GOL model was used to estimate the impact of possible long-run changes in climate. Yield reductions of 5-15 percent from the 2000 levels were postulated for the major areas of the world subject to historically extreme weather fluctuations. These lower yield growth assumptions were run for the Alternative I, the alternative with the higher import demand for the LDCs.

The impact of lower yields would raise prices of wheat by around $24 per ton (1970 dollars). The higher prices would expand area under tillage in those regions capable of expansion to maintain production levels to compensate for lower productivity; they would also curtail grain consumption in importing countries. On balance, the importing countries would import an additional 32 million tons of grain from exporters capable of area expansion, mostly the United States. The higher grain prices would also dampen any rapid expansion of the livestock sector.

Short-Run Fluctuations in Weather and Stock Reserve

The impact of short-run fluctuations in weather on the frequency and magnitude of production shortfalls is examined in the GOL model in terms of the following question: Will maintaining sufficient reserves to meet year to year shortfalls require significantly higher levels of long-run production? Implicit in this question is the assumption that in many parts of the world—particularly in the developing countries—stocks accumulated in bumper years are considerably smaller than would be required to maintain consumption in years of major production shortfall. Policy as well as economic issues would be involved in decisions about the added production needed in years of normal production to provide for needs in shortfall years. Such decisions would need to recognize that long-run grain production levels and grain reserve levels are interrelated.

In any given year, the impact of a "production shortfall" on grain prices is determined by the proportion of the shortfall to be made up through imports and the supplies of grain available to meet resultant changes in world trade. The long-run impact of shortfalls would be reflected by the somewhat higher production levels required over time to maintain planned reserves. The size of this added production would depend on the frequency and magnitude of shortfalls and the policies planned to cope with them.

What is the likelihood of a major shortfall between now and 2000 or in the year 2000? Three major shortfalls occurred during 1950-70, suggesting a probability of about 15 percent in any given year. But if we had considered the period 1960 to date, we could expect two to three shortfalls per decade, or a probability of up to 33 percent that we have a shortfall in any particular year over the projected period. One could also speculate that the frequency and magnitude of shortfalls have increased from minor generally localized disturbances in the 1950s to larger, regionalized shortfalls in the 1960s, and finally to world shortfalls in the decade of the 1970s.

While the five major shortfalls during 1961-75 had many attributes in common, the impact on trade and prices was strikingly different. The following are possible explanations.

The physical production shortfall is not always the relevant shortfall with respect to world trade. Many countries—particularly low-income countries or isolationist trading countries—make up only part of their shortfalls through imports and compensate for the remainder by reducing consumption through direct or indirect price rationing. In 1963 and again in 1965, the USSR, through policies including a deliberate reduction in livestock numbers, made up about a third of their grain production shortfalls at home. But in 1972, the USSR imported a net of 25 million tons of grain in order to maintain growth in livestock production in the face of indigenous shortfall. The USSR might have imported less but for exceptionally low world-market prices. In contrast, even though the USSR grain shortfall was much larger in 1974, world export availabilities were more limited, world market prices were appreciably higher, and Soviet imports were kept limited.

The GOL model (see footnote 1) was used to study the impact of year to year shortfalls as an aberration from Alternative I. The weather impact alternative assumed that production and stock policies are managed to assure stock levels sufficient to meet contingencies assumed in that alternative.

The first set considered the possibility that two major shortfalls during a decade do not occur successively. A recent study (37) suggests that an additional production of 80 million tons over a ten-year period, or 8 million tons of grain production per year, would be required in the early part of the period. This could rise to 10-12 million tons by 2000. Raising annual production levels by this amount in Alternative I has only a minimal effect on long-run average world grain trade prices or quantities traded. World trade prices for wheat as expressed by U.S. export prices would rise only from $80.75 to $83.60 per ton. However, if the frequency of the production shortfalls should double to reach four per decade, world trade prices, as indicated by U.S. gulf port price, would be $87.50 per ton for wheat and $77.00 for corn (1970 dollars)—compared with $80.75 and $74.76 in Alternative I— and the added production needed in round years would increase to 20-25 million tons per year. Thus, it can be concluded that if consistent production and stock policies were implemented, the impact of production shortfalls on long-run production levels would be minimal unless the size of shortfalls or their frequency increased substantially.

However, the above run assumed Alternative I yields and that a production shortfall would not occur two years in succession. If the weather impact alternative had used the lower yield projections reflecting a slower growth of yield because of long-run climatic change, the impact might be significant if pressures against resources already exist even though the weather impact by itself may be minimal. A real resource squeeze in a given year would bring about higher prices and adjustments in grain use such as experienced in 1974. It is also quite likely that, given a series of years in which the world market price of grain continued at high levels, the developing countries would make a special effort to raise production levels through improvements in inputs and the social and institutional organization of agriculture to offset climatic and weather impacts. In any case, the difficult situation probably would not create any more tightness than did the 1972-75 period.

Impact of Expanding Livestock Sector on Cereals Balance in LDCs

The projections suggest that the nature of the food problem facing the less developed world depends to a large extent on a number of demand factors in the developed countries. The amount of grain available to the developing countries over and above their own production—be it in the form of commercial or concessional imports—hinges on the degree to which the developed countries expand, and the developing countries build up, grain-fed livestock sectors.

The grain balances could tighten if certain countries outside of the United States, Canada, and the meat exporters were to accelerate their growth in consumption of livestock products and adopt the grain-intensive feeding techniques of the United States. Food production capacities and income levels are such in the developed countries that there is no question of adequate diets of well over 3,000 calories per day. What is in question, however, is what proportion of these calories will come from grain-fed livestock products and to what extent will the increase in grain feed products raise prices and lower supplies of grain availability to the developing countries.

Consumption of livestock products in the lower-income countries of Western Europe is relatively low; if increases in incomes were to strengthen growth in demand for livestock products substantially, world grain prices could be pushed up as food users in developed countries were forced to bid grain away from feed users. Feed demand in the lower-income developed countries, however, could not be expected to increase substantially unless grains were reasonably priced relative to livestock products.

Much the same case would also be true if even the European Community or Japan attempted to raise livestock protein consumption to levels approaching those prevailing in the United States. In either case, a very affluent developed world could make it harder for the poorer developing countries to raise per capita grain consumption levels much faster than .4 percent per year.

While demand expansion would be difficult without growth in income and population, production and trade policies are likely to be the more important factors determining levels of demand and trade in meats; such policies are particularly important in Western Europe and Japan. Continuation of present policies would indicate a tendency toward high internal prices and continued import barriers. Moreover, a continuation of high oil import costs may cause policymakers in some developed countries to have second thoughts about encouraging per capita meat consumption to grow to current levels in the United States, particularly at the cost of importing large quantities of feed inputs of finished meat products.

Availability of grain at reasonable prices is another important factor in growth of meat demand. The expansion of the livestock industry in the developed countries in the 1960s was made possible largely because of relatively low feed costs. All of our projections indicate that higher feed costs relative to prices received for livestock products are likely. These higher feed costs could dampen expansion of meat production somewhat unless economies were made in feed usage or in the marketing and production structure of the livestock sectors.

The GOL model was used to test the impact on supply-demand cereals balance in the less developed world with relatively low consumption to approach levels of the EC-6. The results indicate $13 per ton rise in corn prices and a $10 rise in world wheat prices. The higher world prices reduce grain imports in the developing world by 9 million tons.

Meeting a substantial increase in demand for grain in the developing countries—whether for food or feed use—will require a sharp increase in these countries' own grain production, and this, in turn, will require an accelerated transfer of technology and inputs from the developed to the developing countries. Progress in improving diets in the developing countries, particularly the amount of animal protein in diets, will also depend on the extent to which these countries restrain population growth. The whole complex of income growth, population growth, technological change in food use, and growth in agricultural and industrial production is closely interrelated.

NEW FRONTIERS

No provision was made under any of the alternatives for the beneficial effect of new technological breakthroughs or for the realization of the full potential of existing agricultural technology in the areas of soil nutrients and plant and animal genetics, among others. Research and development currently in its formative stages and likely to have long gestation periods could well top the unused biological potential of plants and animals in much the same way expanded use of upgraded fertilizers and location-specific hybrids increased corn production in the United States over the last four decades. While there are undoubted natural biological limits on yields imposed by the maximum rate at which plants convert sunlight, carbon dioxide, water, and other nutrients, these natural limits are seldom approached under even the best of circumstances. Despite its crucial importance, this process of photosynthesis is still not fully understood. Efforts to simply realize the potential of the process as it exists now without any improvements could raise food production dramatically (5, 9, 30, 31).

Unforeseen breakthroughs in the energy area would also have a considerable impact on the organization of agriculture and its productivity levels. The long-term beneficial effects of solar and nuclear energy experiments are difficult to project. Inferring from the present state of energy technology, it would appear that large-scale production of electricity and energy-intensive by-products from coal and nuclear sources is the most promising low-cost alternative to use of petroleum. Associated with this type of power production, however, is the generation of heat generally dissipated in water or other liquids. The energy dissipated in heat is actually larger than that converted into electricity. In addition, because of the possibility of radioactive emission, a so-called "exclusion area" or buffer zone around plants might be necessary. Any system which can use this unwanted heat productively could reduce the cost of producing electricity dramatically. One such process might involve "foodplexes," or the introduction of an entirely new food and fiber system based on the energy that would otherwise be wasted (3). These foodplexes could well house integrated sets of activities that would produce—under a controlled environment—a variety of fruit, vegetable, and animal products that otherwise would not be possible. The foodplex would include processing and marketing facilities which, given the location power and foodplexes near large population centers, would reduce per unit transportation costs. Much of the concept of foodplexes is still in the exploratory stage but could well have an impact on the location of the level of production and the direction of trade particularly in commodities which are climate sensitive.

NOTES

[1.] A formal mathematical model, hereafter called the GOL model, designed to capture the interactions of the world grain, oilseeds, and livestock economics is used in this study to project key economic variables to the year 2000. The basic inputs to this model are population and income growth rates, demand and supply price elasticities, input variables, and assumptions about underlying economic trends and policy constraints. The parameters for the mathematical relations were synthesized either from statistical analyses or judgment of experts. For more detailed description of this approach, see larger ERS and ESCS studies in this area (36, 37).

BIBLIOGRAPHICAL NOTES

[1.] Bailey, W. R.; Kutish, F. A. ; and Rojko, A. S. 1974. *Grain Stocks Issues and Alternatives: A Progress Report.* U.S. Department of Agriculture, Economic Research Service, Agriculture Economic Report.

[2.] Baldwin, I. 1970. *A System of Services to Support Agricultural Development.* Bangkok: Asian Agricultural College and University Press.

[3.] Bird, Alan R. 1975. *Foodplexes—Are They a Key to Better Living for All?* U.S. Department of Agriculture, Economic Research Service, working material dated 1 October 1975.

[4.] Blase, Melvin G. 1971. *Institutions in Agricultural Development.* Ames, Iowa: The Iowa State University Press.

[5.] Breimyer, H. F. 1977. The Food-Energy Balance. In *Food Enough or Starvation for Millions,* chapter 16. India: Tata McGraw Hill.

[6.] Brown, Lester. 1975. *By Bread Alone.* New York: Praeger Publishers.

[7.] Brown, Lester. 1974. *In the Human Interest.* Washington, D.C.: Overseas Development Council.

[8.] Buringh, P.; van Heemst, H. D. J.; and Staring, G. J. 1975. Computation of the Absolute Maximum Food Production in the World. Agric. Univ., Dept. Trop. Soil Sci. Netherlands: Wageningen.

9. Bylinsky, Gene. 1975. A New Scientific Effort to Boost Food Output. In *Ag World*, September.

10. Chou, M., and Harmon, D. 1976. Food: Supplying Demand. In *The Next 200 Years*, chapter 5. New York: Morrow and Co.

11. Christensen, R. 1970. *Economic Progress of Agriculture in Developing Nations, 1950-1968.* U.S. Department of Agriculture, Foreign Agricultural Economic Report no. 59.

12. Dalrymple, Dana. 1974. *Development and Spread of High-Yielding Varieties of Wheat and Rice in the Less Developed Countries.* U.S. Department of Agriculture, Foreign Agricultural Economic Report no. 95.

13. Dalrymple, Dana. 1975. *Measuring the Green Revolution: The Impact of Research on Wheat and Rice Production.* U.S. Department of Agriculture, Foreign Agricultural Economic Report no. 106.

14. DeWit, C. T. 1968. Food Production: Past, Present, and Future. Stikostof no. 15, pp. 68-80.

15. Dorner, Peter. 1971. *The Economic Case for Land Reform: Employment, Income Distribution and Productivity.* Madison, Wis.: University of Wisconsin Press, Land Tenure Center.

16. Economic Research Service. 1974. *The World Food Situation and Prospects to 1985.* U.S. Department of Agriculture, Foreign Agriculture Economic Report no. 98.

17. Food and Agriculture Organization. 1970. *Indicative World Plan for Agricultural Development.* Rome.

18. Gasser, William R. 1976. *World Climatic Change and Agriculture — The Issues.* Paper presented at Symposium on Living with Climatic Change, Phase II, 9 November, at Reston, Va.

19. Hanrahan, C. E., and Willett, J. W. 1976. Technology and the World Food Problem — A U.S. View. In *Food Policy*, November, pp. 413-19.

20. International Federation of Institutes for Advanced Study and the Aspen Institute for Humanistic Studies. 1975. *The Policy Implications of Food and Climate Interactions.* Summary of an IFIAS Project Workshop at Aspen, Berlin, 5-7 February.

21. Islam, N. 1974. *Agricultural Policy in Developing Countries.* London: Macmillan Press, Ltd.

22. Kovda, V. A. 1971. The Problem of Biological and Economic Productivity of the Earth's Land Areas. Soviet Geography 12 (1): 6-23.

23. Leith, H., and Whittaker, R. H. 1975. Primary Productivity of the Biosphere. Unpublished draft.

24. McBoyle, Goeffrey. 1973. *Climate in Review.* Boston: Houghton Mifflin Co.

25. McQuigg, J. D. 1977. Effective Use of Weather Information in Projections of

Global Grain Production. In *Food Enough or Starvation for Millions*. India: Tata McGraw Hill.

26. Meadows, Donella H., et al. 1972. *The Limits to Growth: A Report for the Club of Rome's Project on the Predicament of Mankind*. New York: Universe Books.

27. Mesarovic, M., and Pestel, Edward. 1974. *Mankind at the Turning Point: The Second Report to the Club of Rome*. New York: E. P. Dutton, Readers Digest.

28. Mellor, J. W. 1968. The Functions of Agricultural Prices in Economic Development. Ithaca, N. Y.: Department of Agricultural Economics, Cornell University. Reprinted from the *Indian Journal of Agricultural Economics*, vol. 23, no. 1, January-March 1968.

29. Parsons, Kenneth H. 1967. *Institutional Aspects of Agricultural Development*. Reprint Series no. 28. Madison, Wis.: University of Wisconsin Press, Land Tenure Center.

30. *Agricultural Research*. 1975. Raising Biological Ceiling. U.S. Department of Agriculture, September.

31. *Business Week*. 1975. Research to Multiply Food Production: Was Malthus Right? *Business Week*, 16 June.

32. Reutlinger, S., and Selowsky, M. 1976. *Malnutrition and Poverty*. Baltimore, Md.: The Johns Hopkins University Press.

33. Rockefeller Foundation. 1976. Climatic Change, Food Production and Interstate Conflict. Working Papers presented at a conference on climatic change and food production, June 1975 at Bellagio, Italy.

34. Rojko, Anthony S., and O'Brien, Patrick M. 1976. Organizing Agriculture in the Year 2000. *Food Policy*, May, pp. 203-19.

35. Rojko, Anthony S., and O'Brien, Patrick M. 1977. Organizing Agriculture in the Year 2000. In *Food Enough or Starvation for Millions*, chapter 19. India: Tata McGraw Hill.

36. Rojko, Anthony S., and Schwartz, Martin W. 1976. *Modeling the World Grain-Oilseeds-Livestock Economy to Assess World Food Prospects*. Agricultural Economics Research, vol. 28, no. 3, pp. 89-98.

37. Rojko, Anthony S., et al. 1978. Alternative Futures for World Food in 1985. U.S. Department of Agriculture Economics, Statistics, and Cooperatives Service, Foreign Agriculture Economic Report, vol. I, II.

38. Schertz, L. P. 1977. World Needs—Shall the Hungry Be with Us Always? In *Food Policy: U.S. Responsibility in the Life and Death Choices*, chapter 1. Washington, D.C.: The Free Press.

39. Science Council of Canada. 1976. Living with Climatic Change. Proceedings of a Toronto Conference Workshop, 17-22 November 1975, Toronto, Canada.

40. Soil Conservation Service. 1975. Soil Taxonomy: A Basic System of Soil Classifica-

tion for Use in Making and Interpreting Soil Surveys. U.S. Department of Agriculture, Handbook 436.

41. Sterling Forest Conference. 1974. World Food Supply in Changing Climate. Proceedings of Sterling Forest Conference, 2-5 December 1974. Sponsored by American Society of Agronomy and Aspen Institute for Humanistic Studies.

42. United Nations World Food Conference. 1974. Assessment of the World Food Situation Present and Future, 5-16 November 1974, Rome, Italy. (E/CONF 65/3), August.

43. University of California. 1974. *A Hungry World: The Challenge to Agriculture.* Berkeley: University of California Press.

44. U.S. President's Science Advisory Committee. 1967. World Food Problem. Report of the Panel on the World Food Supply, 3 vols., held in May at The White House, Washington, D.C.

45. Willett, Joseph W., ed. 1975. *The World Food Situation: Problems and Prospects to 1985,* 2 vols. Dobbs Ferry, N.Y.: Oceania.

46. Yudelman, Montague. 1971. *Technological Change in Agriculture and Employment in Developing Countries.* Development Centre Studies, Employment Series no. 4.

FOUR

An Overview Of East Asia And Oceania

John F. Shaw

Mr. Shaw joined the Department of Commerce in 1938 as economist and was involved in tariff and trade problems with special attention to Far Eastern countries.

Transferring to the Foreign Service in 1956, he served as First Secretary for Economic Affairs at the American Embassy in Tel Aviv 1957-62; he was assigned to the Trade Agreement Division, including special trade activities from 1962-67. Shaw was a member of U.S. delegations to five different sets of negotiations under the General Agreement on Tariffs (GATT).

Counselor for Commercial Affairs at the American Embassy in Tokyo 1967-71, he then served as Director of Far East Operations, North Texas Commission, 1972-75.

He is President, John Shaw Associates, International Business Consultants.

THE AREA

The countries and lands of the Far East and Oceania which concern this study extend from the Bering Strait and the frozen tundra of eastern Siberia southward across the eastern part of the Asian landmass and the Java Sea to and inclusive of Australia and New Zealand.

In this region are approximately 1.5 billion people—about 37.5 percent of the world's population—living in eighteen major nation states. The land area of the entire region totals 10.3 million square miles—approximately three times the size of the United States. Separating the

United States and East Asia is the vast Pacific Ocean (68.6 million square miles) covering 35 percent of the earth's surface.

The countries and territories of East Asia and Oceania can be grouped into four major categories as follows:

	Land Area (millions of square miles)	Population (millions)
Developed countries	3.1	132.7
Developing countries	1.2	286.5
Developing islands	0.2	3.7
Communist-controlled countries	5.8	993.4
	10.3	1,416.3

They have many things in common but also many dissimilarities. The largest in terms of landmass are mainland China and Australia; the most dispersed are Indonesia (consisting of 13,500 islands extending 3,000 miles) and the Philippines (which consists of 7,100 islands). These latter countries struggle with common problems of communication and transportation.

The population of mainland China (over 900 million) dwarfs that of all of its neighbors combined. In fact, Communist regimes control 70 percent of the population of the region and more than one-half the land area.

On the other hand, the developed countries, which include three countries (Japan, Australia, and New Zealand) with successful democratic political systems, enjoy the highest levels of per capita income and literacy and some of the lowest rates of population growth as seen in Table 4.1. Among the developing countries the largest increase in economic growth is being recorded by Korea, the Philippines, Taiwan, and Indonesia. However, among this group of countries are some of the lowest levels of literacy, the highest rates of population growth, the lowest levels of per capita income, and some of the world's richest sources of foodstuffs, timber, and minerals.

The smallest category in terms of population and land area—but most dispersed—are the "developing islands" consisting of nine island groups in which there are approximately 3.6 million people living on less than 200,000 square miles of land. Some of these are independent sovereign states as noted in Table 4.2.

Climatic conditions range from arctic cold in the Soviet Far East to tropical conditions and abundant rainfall throughout Southeast Asia. Rice is a common staple for many. In the temperate zones, the region is an important source for wheat, feed grains, wool, meat, and dairy products. Significant timber resources are found in Siberia and throughout Southeast Asia. Most of the world's natural rubber comes from Southeast Asia. Important mineral deposits such as coal, lead, zinc, copper, iron ore, bauxite, and tin are found in many countries, as is coal, petroleum, and natural gas. On the other hand, some of the most economically advanced territories such as Japan, Taiwan, Singapore, and Hong Kong are resource poor. (See Table 4.1 for more specific information.)

UNITED STATES' STAKE IN REGION

The United States has historically placed great value on its friendship with the people of East Asia. We have endeavored to be responsive to their political and economic aspirations and have gone to great lengths to establish a security and a commercial framework within which the countries of East Asia can prosper.

Military Costs

In the last twenty-five years, the United States has engaged in two wars in this region—the Korean War and the Vietnam War. The direct cost of these two wars exceeded $137 billion (eleven years in Vietnam—$120 billion, and three years in Korea—$17 billion). In terms of casualties, nearly 80,000 men were killed and 406,000 wounded as is shown in Table 4.3.

What can we expect to happen in the next quarter century? Today there are less than 140,000 troops scattered from Korea to Australia and afloat in units of the Seventh Fleet. This is a marked decline from the peak year of 1969 when 815,000 troops were stationed in East Asia.

In 1976 the largest drop in troop strength from the previous year occurred in Thailand due to the Thai Government's request for complete withdrawal of combat troops. Other cutbacks in the area were due to continued withdrawals of service and support units following the termination of military aid to South Vietnam.

Table 4.1 East Asia and Oceania, 1975

COUNTRIES	LAND AREA (MILLIONS OF SQ. MI)	POPULATION (MILLIONS)	ANNUAL RATE OF GROWTH OF POPULATION	RATE OF LITERACY	PER CAPITA INCOME	GNP (BILLIONS OF DOLLARS)	GNP (REAL GROWTH)	RESOURCES— MAIN EXPORTS
Developed:	**3.1**	**132.7**	**(subtotals)**					
Japan	0.1	110.0	1.2%	98%	$4100	$457.0	6%	Machinery, electronics, automobiles, chemicals, steel
Australia	2.9	13.3	1.6	98.5	4600	41.0	4.9	Cereals, beef, dairy products, minerals
New Zealand	0.1	3.0	1.8	98	3910	11.7	4.8	Mutton, wool, dairy products, beef
Hong Kong	0.	4.2	2.5	75	1300	5.6	8.0	Textiles, electronics, and manufactures
Singapore	0.	2.2	1.4	75	2376	5.3	7	Electrical goods, textiles, ship repairs
Developing Countries:	**1.2**	**286.5**	**(subtotals)**					
China (Taiwan)	0.01	16.1	1.85%	93%	$ 810	14.4	7.8%	Textiles, machinery, plastics, plywood, metal products

Table 4.1 Continued

Indonesia	0.7	139.5	2.1	60	170	14.0	6.7	Petroleum, timber, rubber, tin
Malaysia	0.13	12.1	2.7	50	680	8.7	6	Rubber, palm oil, timber, and rice
Korea	0.05	33.5	1.7	90	480	16.8	10	Textiles, electric machinery, plywood, footwear
Philippines	0.1	43.4	2.9	83	330	10.7	10	Sugar, coconut products, wood, rubber
Thailand	0.2	41.9	2.6	70	310	12.2	3.4	Rice, rubber, corn, wood, tin
Developing Islands:[a]	**0.2**	**3.7**	**2.8%**		**$ 320**			Copra, phosphate, bananas
Communist-Controlled Countries	**5.8**	**993.4**	(subtotals)					
China, PR	3.7	920.0	1.7%	55%[b]	$ 243	223.0	4.7%	Textiles, processed foods, petroleum, light manufactures

Table 4.1 Continued

Country							Exports
Cambodia (Kampuchea)	0.07	7.0	2.2	85ᵇ	70	N.A.	Rice, rubber
Laos, PR	0.09	3.2	2.4	85	70	N.A.	Rice
Vietnam, RP	0.13	41.1	3.0	65	170	N.A.	Rice, corn, tea, coal, chromite
Korea, PR	0.05	15.0	2.8	90	300	N.A.	Rice, corn, metals, machines
Mongolia	0.6	1.3	2.9	N.A.	410	N.A.	Cattle, hides, wool
Siberia, USSR	1.2ᶜ	5.8ᶜ	N.A.	N.A.	N.A.	N.A.	Timber, fish

SOURCES: *U.N. Statistical Year Book*; *World Statistics in Brief*, First Edition; *U.N. Statistical Pocketbook*; Department of Economic and Social Affairs Statistical Office; Statistical Papers Series V, No. 1; also data from background notes on individual countries published by the Department of State.

N.A.: not available
ᵃSee separate table for details.
ᵇClaimed.
ᶜFar Eastern Siberia only.

Table 4.2 Developing Islands: Constitutional Status and Geographical Position

	CONSTITUTIONAL STATUS	AREA[b,c] (KM²)	POPULATION 1971 (THOUSANDS)	RATE OF GROWTH	GNP PER CAPITA 1971
British Solomon Islands	British protectorate	28,446	168	2.6	$200
Cook Islands	New Zealand dependency with internal self-government	238[d]	21	2.1	475
Fiji	Independent dominion	18,272	530	2.5	470
Gilbert and Ellice Islands	British Crown Colony	886	60	1.9	470
Naura	Independent republic; member of Commonwealth	21	7[f]	[5.5][a]	N.A.
Papua New Guinea	Independent sovereign nation	461,691[e]	2,520	2.8	320
Tonga	Constitutional monarchy	549	90	3.0	300
Trust Territory of the Pacific Islands	United Nations Trust Territory administered by U.S.A.	1,799[e]	110	2.9	390
Western Samoa	Independent sovereign state	2,842	146	2.4	140
Total		514,724[g]	3,652		

SOURCES: UNCTAD, *Developing Island Countries:Report of the Panel of Experts* (TD/B/443/Rev.1), July 1973; United Nations/UNCTAD, South Pacific Regional Transport Survey, July 1972; The Mercantile Marine Atlas.
N.A.: not available   [a]Figures in brackets are estimates.   [b]Land Territory in km² includes interisland waters.   [c]Unless otherwise specified, area estimates include inland waters.   [d]Land area.   [e]Inhabited dry land area only.   [f]1970.   [g]1 sq. kil. = 0.386 square miles.

Table 4.3   The Cost of America's Recent Wars in Asia

	VIETNAM WAR (11 YEARS)	KOREAN WAR (3 YEARS)
Peak Buildup of Troops in War Zone	543,400	327,000
Casualties		
Killed in Combat	45,619	33,629
Wounded in Combat	302,393	103,284
DIRECT COST OF WAR	$120 billion	$17 Billion

SOURCE: *U.S. News & World Report,* 3 January 1972, p. 20.

Security System

The United States military presence in East Asia is made possible by a series of agreements dating from the end of World War II which provide this country with a number of military bases. Also as part of this security system is a series of mutual defense assistance agreements which commit the United States to come to the aid of our East Asian friends in case they should be subject to external attack. In the north the United States has bilateral agreements with Korea and Japan, and in the central region with Taiwan and the Philippines; it has base privileges with all four. In Southeast Asia the United States also has a collective security arrangement called SEATO with the Philippines, Thailand, Pakistan, Australia, New Zealand, France, and the United Kingdom. In the south, a somewhat earlier collective security arrangement in effect with Australia and New Zealand is referred to as ANZUS; this remains the cornerstone of our relationship with these two countries and provides commitments in case of an attack on any of them or on the U.S. in the Pacific area.

The United States enjoys base privileges in Korea, Japan, Taiwan, and the Phillipines. Currently the United States is negotiating a new base agreement with the government of the Philippines which reportedly would provide payments of $1 billion evenly divided between economic and military aid to the Philippines for continued use of the bases there for the next five years. The outcome of these negotiations are important to our continued presence and operations at Clark Air Base and Subic Bay Naval Station.

Further to the south and east a newcomer to Oceania has surfaced: the Soviet Union has recently asked Western Samoa for permission to establish a fishing base, a move of concern to some observers since Western Samoa is only 80 miles from American Samoa and 3000 miles to the northwest lies United States' positions in Guam and the northern Marianas. The Soviets are also reported to have made a similar offer to the Kingdom of Tonga a few hundred miles to the south; in addition, a Soviet-built international airport has been offered to this island kingdom.[1]

Foreign Aid

To promote the military, political, and economic strength of our friends in East Asia we have given generous financial support. The sum total of loans and grants to countries of East Asia from 1946 to 1975 comes to more than $60 billion: $35 billion in military assistance and $25 billion in economic assistance. During this same period Oceania received $738.2 million in aid as a group. East Asia and Oceania account for one-third of all military and economic aid given by the United States to all countries since the end of World War II.[2]

Overall aid expenditures in East Asia have declined sharply on an annual basis since 1973—U.S. military operations ceased in Vietnam early in that year—dropping from $5.8 billion to $1.9 billion in 1975. In fiscal year 1975 nine countries were beneficiaries of some form of assistance. Although aid to Cambodia, Laos, and Vietnam did terminate in that year, the area received $621 million in economic assistance and $1.2 billion in military aid, half of which was on a grant basis as detailed in Table 4.4. Aid to Oceania in that year totalled $4.3 million and financed primarily Peace Corp activities.

UNITED STATES AID—FY1975: OCEANIA
(thousands of dollars)

Gilbert & Ellis Islands	$21.0
Fiji	944.0
Solomons	115.0
Micronesia	1,875.0
Tonga	455.0
Western Samoa	930.0
Total	$4,340.0

Table 4.4 U.S. Aid[a]—FY1975: East Asia (millions of dollars)

	CAMBODIA[b]	CHINA REPUBLIC OF	HONG KONG	INDONESIA	KOREA	LAOS[c]	MALAYSIA	PHILIPPINES	SINGAPORE	THAILAND	VIETNAM[d]	TOTAL
Economic Assistance												
Total (AID, Food for Peace, Peace Corps and Other)	149.0	NIL*	NIL	89.8	36.7	26.5	2.9	68.5	NIL	6.7	240.9	621.0
Loans	91.5			69.9	27.2	—	—	45.0		NIL	45.7	279.3
Grants	57.5			19.9	9.5[f]	26.5	2.9	23.5		6.7	195.2	341.7
Military Assistance												
Total	256.0	82.7	NIL	21.0	144.7	19.9	5.0	36.3	NIL	42.5	625.1	1,233.2
Credits or Loans	—	80.0		5.0	59.0	—	4.7	14.0		8.0	—	170.7
Grants	256.0	2.7[e]		16.0	85.7	19.9	0.3	22.3		34.5	625.1	1,062.5
Total Economic and Military Aid	405.0	82.7	NIL	110.8	181.4	46.4	7.9	104.8	NIL	49.2	866.0	1,854.2
Credits or Loans	91.5	80.0		74.9	86.2	—	4.7	59.0		8.0	45.7	450.0
Grants	313.5	2.7		35.9	95.2	46.4	3.2	45.8		41.2	820.3	1,404.2
Other U.S. Loans and Grants (largely Export-Import Bank Loans)	NIL	190.2	5.5	211.2	293.0	NIL	34.6	24.9	20.2	3.3	NIL	782.9

SOURCE: U.S. Overseas Loans and Grants; Obligations and Loan Authorizations, July 1, 1945-June 30, 1975, AID, Department of State.

[a]Obligations and loan authorizations. [b]Aid terminated. [c]Aid terminated. [d]Aid terminated. [e]Grant military aid now terminated. [f]Grant economic aid terminated at end of FY75. *NIL: None.

FY-1977. The proposed FY77 aid program for East Asia and Oceania totals $834 million—less than half the size of the FY75 program. Out of the total aid package, $334 million is earmarked for economic assistance with $499.8 million for military aid. The bulk of the planned economic aid will go to China (Taiwan), Korea, and the Philippines largely under the food aid sales programs (Public Law 480). These provide for the sale of agricultural commodities on credit terms payable in United States dollars or local currency. The planned military aid program of $499.8 million is for Korea, Indonesia, Philippines, Malaysia, and China (Taiwan) under loan programs; grant military aid is less than 15 percent of the total. Korea is to receive more than one-half of the total military aid program as is evident in Table 4.5.

Other. East Asia has also received extensive bilateral aid from other countries, e.g., Japan, Australia, United Kingdom, West Germany, and from international institutions such as the World Bank and the Asian Development Bank. The World Bank, for example, loaned nearly $1 billion to borrowers in East Asia and the Pacific in 1975, with a proposed $1,458,500,000 loan in 1976.[3] These are significant increases from the annual lending rate of $381 million for this region in the years 1969-73.

Loans of the World Bank outstanding in East Asia as of June 30, 1976, totalled $4.5 billion—about 20 percent of the Bank's loans to all countries.[4]

United States Trade

Since World War II, United States trade with East Asia has skyrocketed from a two-way level (exports and imports combined) of $2.5 billion in 1950 to $42.2 billion in 1975.

Japan today is the largest market for the United States in Asia and also this country's largest overseas market worldwide. Exports to Japan reached their highest level in the past quarter century in 1974 at $10.7 billion of which two-thirds consisted of agricultural commodities and industrial raw materials; imports from Japan in 1974 worth $12.3 billion were also at a record high. As evidenced from Table 4.6, a slight drop occurred in the level of both exports and imports in 1975.

United States trade with the other developed countries of East Asia and Oceania is also significant. As a group (Japan included) these

Table 4.5   East Asia-Oceania: U.S. Economic Assistance, Military Assistance, and Credit Sales Programs Proposed for FY 1977
(in thousands of dollars)

		Economic Assistance Programs					Military Assistance Programs				
	TOTAL ECONOMIC & MILITARY ASSISTANCE	TOTAL ECONOMIC ASSISTANCE	A.I.D.	PEACE CORPS	P.L. 480	INT'L NARCOTICS CONTROL	TOTAL MILITARY ASSISTANCE	MILITARY ASSISTANCE GRANTS (MAP)	FOREIGN MILITARY TRAINING	FOREIGN MILITARY CREDIT SALES	EXCESS DEFENSE ARTICLES
East Asia: Total	828,605	328,805	104,800	7,981	214,614	1,410	499,800	67,700	8,600	419,100	4,400
China (Taiwan)	35,900	—	—	—	—	—	35,900	400	500	35,000	—
Indonesia	137,636	91,536	49,900	—	41,561	75	46,100	19,400	3,000	23,100	600
Korea	432,885	146,885	—	1,851	145,034	—	286,000	8,300	2,700	275,000	—
Malaysia	38,478	2,178	—	2,178	—	—	36,300	—	300	36,000	—
Philippines	115,793	74,393	44,100	2,329	27,964	—	41,400	19,600	600	20,000	1,200
Singapore	55	55	—	55	—	—	—	—	—	—	—
Thailand	67,858	13,758	10,800	1,623	—	1,335	54,100	20,000	1,500	30,000	2,600
OCEANIA: TOTAL	5,129	5,129	—	5,017	112	—	—	—	—	—	—
British Solomon Islands	731	731	—	619	112	—	—	—	—	—	—
Fiji	1,238	1,238	—	1,238	—	—	—	—	—	—	—
Gilbert & Ellice Islands	28	28	—	28	—	—	—	—	—	—	—
Micronesia	1,526	1,526	—	1,526	—	—	—	—	—	—	—
Tonga	687	687	—	687	—	—	—	—	—	—	—
Western Samoa	919	919	—	919	—	—	—	—	—	—	—

SOURCE: Agency for International Development Fiscal Year 1977; Submission to the Congress: Asia Programs, February 1976.

countries currently account for 67 percent of total United States trade with this area; in 1950 they accounted for only 42 percent.

Among the developing countries, trade with China (Taiwan), Korea, and Indonesia is the largest, followed by the Philippines, Malaysia, and Thailand.

Table 4.6   United States Trade with Countries of Far East and Oceania

(millions of dollars)

COUNTRIES	1950		1975	
	EXPORTS	IMPORTS	EXPORTS	IMPORTS
Developed countries	$ 666.3	$ 393.0	$13,594	$14,767.
Australia	115.1	141.1	1,816.	1,147.
New Zealand	29.4	64.5	411.	245.
Hong Kong	103.5	5.4	808.	1,575.
Japan	418.3	182.0	9,565.	11,268.
Singapore	n.s.a.*	n.s.a.	994.	532.
Developing countries	$ 445.9	$ 782.5	$ 5,815.	$ 7,322.
China (Taiwan)	40.3	3.3	1,660.	1,938.
Indonesia	84.9	155.7	810.	2,221.
Malaysia	21.3	310.0	395.	776.
Korea	23.3	2.3	1,761.	1,416.
Philippines	247.0	236.0	832.	754.
Thailand	29.1	75.2	357.	217.
Communist-controlled countries	$ 73.1	$ 157.6	$ 587.	$ 164.
Cambodia	]		66.	
Laos	] 27.4	11.1	4.	b
Vietnam	]		213.	6.
North Korea	]		NIL†	NIL
Mongolia	] 45.7a	146.5a	b	NIL
Siberia, USSR	]		n.s.a.	n.s.a.
China, P.R.	]		304.	157.
Total for the region	$1,185.3	$1,333.1	$19,996.	$22,253.

SOURCE: Bureau of Census, 1950, 1975.

*n.s.a.: not separately available.
†NIL: none.
a Communist area in Asia.
b Less than $500,000.

United States trade with the Communist-controlled countries, including mainland China, totaling $751 million in 1975 is miniscule; this is less than 2 percent of all our trade with the region as shown in Table 4.6.

While the situation varies from country to country, in many instances the United States is supplying from 20-25 percent of total imports and receives from 25 to 35 percent of all exports shipped from the countries of East Asia. In a very real sense South Korea, China (Taiwan), Japan, and Hong Kong have become workshops of the United States and heavily dependent on the health of the United States economy.

United States Investments

Given the strong United States military presence and extensive foreign aid programs, the United States and other foreign countries private investments and trade with East Asia have flourished. As of 1975, overall United States investments in this region totalled nearly $14 billion. Most of this has taken place in the developed countries of Australia and Japan and centered in such activities as manufacturing, mining, and petroleum. Among the developing countries, Indonesia and the Philippines have been attractive to investors as is evident from Table 4.7.

Figures are not readily available on direct investments of all other developed countries in East Asia and Oceania economies. In most instances, Japan has increasingly become a very important source of private investments funds for most countries of this region. Japan's direct investments in this region are estimated at nearly $5 billion—concentrated in resource development, import substitution, and export-oriented activities.

WHAT TO EXPECT (1976-99)

The problems confronting mankind over the next twenty-five years will be made up largely from those matters which have already emerged and on which we are now at work. These include such global issues as food, energy, raw materials, trade, technology, the environment, and use of the ocean and outer space. Some of these problems

Table 4.7 U.S. Investments in the Far East and Oceania, 1975
(millions of dollars)

COUNTRIES	ALL INDUSTRIES	MINING	PETROLEUM	MANUFACTURING	TRANSPORTATION	TRADE	FINANCE	OTHER
Developed:	$9886	N.A.	N.A.	N.A.	N.A.	N.A.	N.A.	N.A.
Japan	3328	NIL†	1314	1564	35	291	76	48
Australia	5090	1063	888	2367	−2	326	286	162
New Zealand	368	N.A.	139	116	—	53	N.A.	43
Hong Kong	500(e)							
Singapore	600(e)							
Developing Countries:	$3795	N.A.	N.A.	N.A.	N.A.	N.A.	N.A.	N.A.
China (Taiwan)	500(e)							
Indonesia	1612	N.A.	1298	94	11	N.A.	5	50
Malaysia	400(e)							
Korea	250(e)							
Philippines	733	N.A.	135	339	26	100	68	N.A.
Thailand	300(e)							

SOURCES: U.S. Department of Commerce: *Survey of Current Business; Overseas Business Reports,* etc.

(e) Estimates from Overseas Business Reports and other Department of Commerce sources.
N.A.: not available.
†NIL: none.

will require new institutions. Most will be handled within a multilateral framework and all will involve the United States and the countries of East Asia and Oceania in varying ways. Let us examine a few as they apply to this region.

Food

While population growth rates in the developed countries will be falling and a stable state of population reached around the year 2000, the last quarter of this century will still see high rates of population growth in the developing countries — *rates which in recent years have exceeded the percent of growth of food output per head, according to United Nations sources.*[5] Thus the pressure upon the world's food-producing potential will remain enormous throughout this period.

The outlook is further clouded by some experts among the world climatologists who are predicting that major droughts are likely to occur by 1990; they believe the world's climate is not getting better and could become more variable in our crop-growing areas than in recent years. Further, there are experts who believe that areas in the high latitudes both north and south of the equator have started to cool off rather than warm: this would reduce growing seasons and rainfall in central Canada, Russia and China. Tropical regions would be hit by frequent droughts, particularly in southern and western Africa where rain is already scarce. Some grain-importing countries are planning ahead for shortages by increasing stockpiling facilities. Japan, for example, having been shocked by the United States embargo on soybean shipments three years ago, is expanding domestic storage facilities on a limited basis and developing alternative sources of supply, such as Brazil.

The World Food Council, formed following the World Food Conference in November 1974 as a permanent body of the United Nations, is actively pursuing food strategies and calling for doubling annual investment in agriculture in developing countries in the second half of the 1970s. In terms of 1976 currency values, this probably means annual investments of around $10 billion a year from developed countries.[6] In this connection, it should be noted that in a recent report on Japan's overseas investments, Japan's External Trade Organization suggested that Japanese firms should consider the agribusiness area in developing nations as a potential for new investments.

Asian and African states are expected to benefit from a second United Nations effort to expand food output—the International Fund for Agricultural Development (IFAD) of $1 billion, which is to become operative early this year.[7] The petroleum exporting countries of the OPEC are the largest contributors ($435.5 million); however, the United States made the largest single pledge of $200 million. The fund is unique in that the developing countries will have a two-thirds majority in fund decisions. Asia, which is providing only 7 percent of IFAD financing might expect to receive well over 30 percent of the fund's resources.[8]

Included in the World Food Council's provisional list of forty-three food priority countries are eleven Asian nations, of which two— Indonesia and the Philippines—are in East Asia. In the absence of significant improvements, Indonesia's deficit as a percentage of 1985 consumption requirements may amount to 27 percent and the Philippine deficit may amount to 17 percent.

Fortunately, as this quarter century begins, the worldwide food outlook is showing the first real improvement since 1972. According to figures released by the United Nations Food and Agricultural Organization (FAO) on November 29, 1976, world food production rose 2 percent in 1975 and increased about 4 percent in developing countries. Output in the Far East rose 8 percent; this was considered very satisfactory.[9]

For 1976, the FAO reported that a further production increase of 2 to 3 percent is expected in both developed and developing countries. However, the report concluded that production for the decade of the 1970s so far was well below targets adopted by the United Nations.

Raw Materials

East Asia and Oceania are rich in mineral resources and other raw materials which are increasingly coming into short supply. In fact, a United Nations-sponsored study on "The Future of the World Economy" states that between 1970 and 2000 "the demand for copper is expected to increase 4.8 times, for bauxite and zinc 4.2 times, nickel 4.3 times, lead 5.3 times, iron ore 4.7 times, petroleum 5.2 times, natural gas 4.5 times and coal 5.0 times," while predicting that only lead and zinc are likely to run out by the turn of the century. The report noted that other experts in this field have expressed concern about the adequacies of such other minerals as asbestos, fluorine, gold, mercury, phosphorous, silver, tin, and tungsten. The report goes on to say that "the world is expected to consume during the last thirty years of the twentieth century from three to four times as many minerals as have been consumed throughout the whole previous history of civilization.[10]Clearly there is a growing worldwide dependence on the untapped raw materials of East Asia and Oceania.

Without attempting to catalogue all the mineral wealth in this region, let me cite just one example, uranium. Australia is believed to have more uranium than any other country in the non-Communist world. Proven reserves are placed at 30 percent of the world's known supply; most of this was discovered in the late 1960s. Australia has signed firm contracts with utilities and government agencies in the United States, Japan, and West Germany for deliveries to begin in 1977. These exports could be earning Australia $2 billion a year by the early eighties.[11]

Petroleum and natural gas are also found in significant amounts throughout much of the area. For example, the USSR has been discussing the construction of pipelines with Japan to move supplies of oil and natural gas from its vast fields in Tyumen in northwestern Siberia and Yakutsk in northeastern Siberia to Pacific ports for eventual transshipment to Japan and the United States. Other significant quantities of oil are found in China and Indonesia.[12] Approximately 2 percent of the world's reserves are in Indonesia. Today it is the fifth ranking supplier of petroleum to the United States. In the energy-deficit areas an intensive search for new deposits of gas and oil is under way, e.g., in Japan, Korea, the Philippines, and Thailand.

The importance which developing countries attach to the foreign exchange earned from the export of their resources to world markets cannot be minimized. These minerals and the products of their fields and forests provide the key to industrialization, decent incomes, and better diets. Their growth and prosperity depend in large measure on maximizing their earnings from these exports. However, these export earnings are subject to the whims of weather, swings in worldwide demand, and availability of technology and investment capital.

At the fourth ministerial meeting of the United Nations Conference on Trade and Development held on May 6, 1976 in Nairobi, the United States attempted to come to grips with the problems and aspirations of the developing countries. Secretary Kissinger proposed the establishment of an International Resources Bank (IRB). This new institution would promote "more rational, systematic and equitable development of resources in developing nations. It would facilitate technological development and management training. It would help ensure supplies of raw materials to sustain the expansion of the global economy and help moderate commodity price fluctuations."[13] The Bank would commence operations with a capital fund of $1 billion. Among other things, the Bank would participate with foreign investors and the host governments in specifying mutually acceptable conditions of investment and would aid in working out formulas for production sharing and in training and supporting the transfer of technology and building up marketing capabilities in the host country.

On the subject of raw material commodity trade, the Secretary said, "There are a number of ways to improve commodity markets—long term contractual arrangements, better exchange of market information, improved distribution, more efficient production methods and better storage and transport facilities."[14] He recognized that in some situations buffer stocks deserved to be considered and in the absence of other sources of financing the IRB might offer a supplemental channel.

To date no concensus has evolved between the producers of primary raw material and the developed countries on methods of avoiding drastic price changes which disrupt foreign exchange earnings and development plans.

Clearly, however, some new international trading arrangement can be expected to emerge in the next several years to cope with this problem.

Environment

The developed countries of this region are increasingly involved in programs to protect and to clean up the environment. Japan, for example, has had comprehensive environmental pollution control laws since 1967. These laws, which were strengthened in 1970, cover air pollution, water pollution, and noise standards; enforcement of most of these controls rests with the prefectural and local governments. Approval of building sites for nuclear power plants, as well as industrial and chemical plants, must be obtained from local authorities and this is no longer readily granted. Japanese communities are now very much aware of public hazards from industrial wastes. The prevalence of mercury poisoning cases (Minamata Disease), of cadmium poisoning (Itai-Itai-Byo-aching diseases), and of Yokkaichi (asthma and other troubles) is well publicized.

Whereas Japan was not greatly concerned about its environment prior to 1970, this is not true today. For example, Tokyo's new $750 million international airport at Narita continues to stand idle four years after completion due to vigorous opposition from local farmers, environmentalists, and student sympathizers. As for industries, the steel makers perhaps best illustrate what is occurring in industrial sectors: in 1975 this industry spent 18.7 percent of its total capital expenditures on environmental protection.

Increasingly Japanese industrialists are turning to the developing countries of East Asia and Oceania as possible sites for new plant investments. But these investments are not always welcomed in the underdeveloped areas. For example, Singapore, Malaysia, and Indonesia are working on new traffic regulations which may bar the mammoth oil tankers from the narrow and shallow Straits of Malacca. As an alternative, a new route passing south of Indonesia and then through the Lombok Strait and the Makassar Strait to a proposed supertanker port in the Palau Islands is being considered. The development of a deep water port in this thinly populated area (13,000 people) could result in a multimillion dollar complex of refining and smelting activities. While Palau's elected leaders are nearly unanimous in their support for the project, vocal opposition is developing from the Save Palau Association. Members of this association fear the port will overwhelm Palau with outsiders since the skills needed to run the port are not available locally and possibly as many as 12,000 people may have to be brought in. They reason "Our fathers saved Palau for us and we should do the same for the next generation."[15]

Ocean Development

A new area for resource development is the oceans. Modern technology is enabling mankind to reach great depths (as well as higher altitudes) and will in the next quarter century bring about many new opportunities and challenges for businesses, for governments, and for international cooperation.

Presently, we are able to drill for oil farther off shore than ever before, to exploit living resources of the ocean more efficiently, and to carry crude oil in electronically controlled tankers; soon we will be able to mine for minerals in deep sea beds.

No nation in Asia has been more dependent on the sea and consequently more interested in these developments than Japan. Given its deficiencies in foodstuffs, particularly in proteins and minerals, Japan has much at stake in how the international community proceeds to control developments over 70 percent of the earth's surface.

Currently an effort is underway at the United Nations to establish a legal regime for the development of the oceans, referred to as the Law of the Sea. These negotiations are aimed at establishing an order for the oceans that will prevent, or resolve peacefully, conflict over the uses of the oceans among more than 150 nations. The proposed convention sets forth broad obligations and responsibilities on the part of both maritime and coastal powers to preserve the ocean's integrity and to cooperate with countries in protecting the oceans from pollution.

Secretary Kissinger presented a package proposal in 1976 to resolve the outstanding issues dealing with mining for mineral nodules on the ocean floor. Individual nations and their companies would have assured access to mining sites, along with an international "enterprise" which would be an arm of the proposed Seabed Authority. We and other countries are willing to assist this international enterprise in a broadly shared financing and staffing of its intended operations with the understanding that all nations would also have assured access to the seabed.[16]

Pending the completion of this broadly based treaty, the United States is actively negotiating a series of bilateral agreements with those countries that fish in United States waters which recognize that the United States has established a fishery conservation zone within 200 nautical miles of its coast. Under these agreements, the United States will determine the allowable catch that will be available to foreign fishing vessels and will use a system of permits which set forth the terms and conditions under which the catch is available. Agreements were concluded in September and November 1976 with China (Taiwan) and the USSR and are under negotiation with Japan and South Korea. Under this program the United States set March 1, 1977, for extending this country's fishing limit from twelve to 200 miles. Japan and Korea, both of which adhere to a twelve-mile limit, finally agreed in December of 1976 to accept the United States decision to extend its fishery jurisdiction. This change in position was facilitated when the Soviets announced they too were extending the USSR jurisdiction to 200 miles.

In the event the Law of the Sea Treaty is adopted and the United States signs the treaty and there is a discrepancy between the bilateral fisheries agreements and the treaty—for example, as regards the 200-nautical-mile ocean jurisdiction—then the treaty provisions will take precedence.

The last quarter of this century will continue to see new multilateral and bilateral arrangements affecting fishing and mining rights of the countries bordering on the Pacific Ocean.

The scope of the economic matters described above is not limited to any given region, e.g., East Asia, and the matters are not such that they can be resolved by a single state or a small group of states. They are global in nature and involve both industrial and developing countries.

At the moment throughout the Free World great sensitivity is being evidenced by all United States trading partners to the plans of the new administration which has taken over in Washington. National policies are in abeyance waiting for the United States to set its policies regarding oil prices, energy policy, raw materials, relations with third-world countries, and not the least, United States domestic programs and their effectiveness in promoting economic growth. Certainly, United States' friends in Asia know that their economic measures are going to depend greatly on the American market and its impact on world trade.

Trade

To facilitate economic growth in the free world and particularly in the developing countries, the United States will continue its historical program of reducing global trade barriers for the next quarter century. These tariff reduction measures date back prior to World War II and moved to a multilateral framework in the General Agreement on

Tariffs and Trade in 1947. Since then a series of multilateral agreements have been concluded which greatly benefited postwar recovery and, in modern times, the economic growth and stability of countries in East Asia, for example, Japan, South Korea, China (Taiwan), Hong Kong, and Singapore.

Currently the United States is involved in multilateral trade negotiations in Geneva, known as the Tokyo Round. These are targeted to be completed by the end of 1977. In these negotiations we are keeping in mind the special trade needs of developing countries, especially as they relate to processed goods which are important to industrial development, particularly in the poorer nations of the world, as well as to improving conditions of trade for tropical products.

In January 1976, the United States instituted a system of generalized tariff preferences (GSP) which have opened up significant new trading opportunities for developing nations. Other major industrial nations have similar preferential arrangements. Our own system covers more than 2,700 items from nearly 100 countries. The annual trade value of these items is roughly $2.5 billion. In East Asia certain imports from Hong Kong, Thailand, Indonesia, and the Philippines are benefiting. The United States is examining the possibility of including additional products.

The importance of reducing tariffs against the import of processed raw materials and manufactures from developing nations cannot be minimized from the standpoint of the contribution this makes to growth and economic development. In the last quarter century we have seen five great industrial centers emerge in Asia—Japan, South Korea, China (Taiwan), Hong Kong, and Singapore. In the next quarter century Indonesia, the Philippines, Thailand, and Malaysia will be seeking similar achievements.

This growth, as it always has in the past, will be accompanied with dislocations in the markets of the developed countries. Currently Japanese imports of steel, television sets, and automobiles are troublesome to U.S. manufacturers; textiles from Hong Kong, South Korea, and Taiwan are being attacked by domestic garment makers, including the rank and file of the International Ladies Garment Workers. U.S. shoe manufacturers are already asking the new administration in Washington to limit shoe imports by a system of quotas.

Over the next quarter century, domestic interests can be expected to continue to exert pressure to exclude imports from the emerging nations which are disruptive to U.S. manufacturer's markets. Should there be a significant buildup in textile manufacturing for export in mainland China and India then these countries are likely to be the new targets.

Despite short-term reverses the overall level of United States trade with East Asia and Oceania will continue to rise as the resources of the region are further developed, as the purchasing power of the Asian worker rises, and as new plants and industries emerge.

Throughout Southeast Asia, United States suppliers of agribusiness, food processing, mining, construction, and other plant equipment, as well as educational and medical suppliers, should do well in the next decade. In the developed countries import demand may move to more sophisticated industrial items. In these nations there is concern over water and waste pollution, noise control, the environment, new and clean sources of energy, mining of the oceans, and searching in outerspace. In addition, given high levels of per capita income, consumer expectations will be strong for quality goods. In this situation the long-term United States sales prospects are good for noise and vibration abatement equipment; lasers and electro-optical equipment, computers, peripherals, and data communications equipment; process control equipment; analytical instruments; testing-measuring equipment for electronic industry; electronic computer software; biomedical equipment; hydraulic equipment and components; mechanical handling equipment; building systems and materials, and high quality and unique consumer goods of all kinds.

While forecasting is risky, it is interesting to speculate that two-way trade between the United States and East Asia and Oceania might total nearly $710 billion by the year 2000—if it were to increase from its 1975 level of $42.2 billion at the same rate United States trade increased with this region between 1950 and 1975.

Finance

To finance development goals and to pay for imports, most countries of East Asia are borrowing heavily from international institutions, foreign governments, and private commercial institutions as pointed out in the section on foreign aid.

Future needs are also staggering. Examples follow.

South Korea: Expected inflow of funds from all foreign sources in 1976 is estimated at $2.1 billion. It seeks capital inflow of $10 billion during 1977-81.

China: Annual borrowing needs through the seventies
(Taiwan) amount to $400-$500 million annually.

Indonesia: Expected inflow of capital funds in 1976 is estimated at $3.4 billion.

Thailand: Expected inflow of capital funds in 1976 is estimated at $773 million.

Philippines: Expected inflow of capital funds in 1976 is estimated at $700 million.[17]

This borrowing is resulting in a growing external debt burden which in East Asia and Oceania now exceeds $23.7 billion. The debt figures in Table 4.8 are not inclusive of all outstanding debt and in many countries (e.g., Indonesia), little is known of the private sector borrowing.

**Table 4.8   East Asia and Oceania Total External Debt
Outstanding—December 31,1974
(billions of United States dollars)**

COUNTRIES	AMOUNT[*]
China (Taiwan)	$ 2.6
Fiji	0.1
Indonesia	8.7
South Korea	6.1
Malaysia	2.2
Philippines	2.0
Singapore	0.6
South Vietnam	0.3
Thailand	1.1
Total	**$23.7**

SOURCE: World Bank, *Annual Report 1976,* p. 102.

[*] Includes undisbursed funds.

The heavy borrowings in this region will be a cause of continuing concern for the next several years because of fear that the external debts of some countries may grow so large that merely to pay the interest on the debt will become too great a burden for some. This may also become a concern of foreign banks which find themselves in trouble because of loans outstanding and on which repayment must be delayed.

In the case of the Philippines, the debt-service burden amounted to 16 percent in 1976 and will rise to 17.9 percent in 1980. The debt-service ratio in the case of South Korea is scheduled to peak at 13.8 percent in 1977. The projection for Indonesia is that the debt-service ratio will peak in 1979 at 19.5 percent.

This debt problem is aggravated by any rise in import costs and—except for Indonesia and Malaysia—will not be eased by an increase in the cost of petroleum; it is also aggravated by any downturn in industrial activity in major industrial markets into which the raw materials and manufactures from the developing countries are sold.

Some major institutional effort may be needed to solve the debt-service problems of several East Asian countries if they are unable to sell the goods and services which they are capable of producing in world markets. Their economic well-being and political stability are highly dependent upon a global community free of trade barriers and in which economic growth is expanding.

Political

The economic issues which concern the United States and its friends in East Asia and Oceania and which have been considered above are not geographically peculiar to this region. They are, in most instances, representative of worldwide problems.

On the other hand, there are several political matters peculiar to East Asia and which may be of concern to United States policymakers for many years to come.

Vietnam.   United States military involvement in this area initially ended with the signing on January 27, 1973, of the Agreement on Ending the War and Restoring Peace in Vietnam, and then ultimately with the fall of the Saigon Government in 1975. Today Communist regimes are in control of Vietnam, Cambodia, and Laos. The United

States retains a mission in Laos but has no representatives in either Vietnam or Cambodia.

Vietnam has been forcibly unified under a totalitarian regime. Similar regimes have taken over in the other countries; all three are preoccupied with internal matters. Relations with one another and bordering states are confused—as are Hanoi's longer-term ambitions.

The United States has indicated a willingness to open discussions with Vietnamese authorities, with both sides free to raise any issues. Exploratory talks occurred late last year in Paris. In addition, the House Select Committee on Americans Missing in Southeast Asia has also recently requested the administration to enter into serious negotiations with these states aimed at normalizing relations.[18]

There appears to be no insurmountable problems to a steady improvement of ties with Vietnam, Cambodia, and Laos. The United States stands ready to reciprocate gestures of goodwill, and I thoroughly expect an early resumption of diplomatic relations and the reestablishment of commercial ties, including an extension of most-favored-nation treatment to these countries.

Korea.   The next quarter century will see the United States taking new initiatives to ease tensions on the Korean peninsula. Former Secretary Kissinger frequently called attention to the threat to world peace and security occasioned by the confrontation between North and South Korea. Speaking to the United Nations General Assembly September 30, 1976, he said:

> Our own views on the problem of Korea are well known. We have called for a resumption of a serious dialogue between North and South Korea. We have urged wider negotiations to promote security and reduce tensions. We are prepared to have the United Nations Command dissolved so long as the Armistice Agreement—which is the only existing legal arrangement committing the parties to keep the peace—is either preserved or replaced by more durable arrangements. We are willing to improve relations with North Korea, provided that its allies are ready to take similar steps toward the Republic of Korea. We are ready to talk with North Korea about the Peninsula's future, but we will not do so without the participation of the Republic of Korea.

To achieve this goal he has repeatedly called for a conference including all the parties most directly concerned—North and South Korea, the United States, and the People's Republic of China—to discuss ways of adapting the Armistice Agreement to new conditions and replacing it with more permanent arrangements.

The United States continues to wait for South Korea and other concerned parties to evidence interest in this or some other constructive proposal. Meanwhile, the leadership of United States foreign policy has come into new hands. President Carter said during the political campaign that he would withdraw nuclear weapons and reduce United States ground forces in South Korea. Melvin R. Laird, former Secretary of Defense (1969-72), is said to believe the United States should pull its ground troops out of South Korea but leave its air power there.[19]

According to a press account, the principal elements of the 42,000-man American force in South Korea are a 12,500 strong infantry division, a missile unit with nuclear potential, an air defense brigade, and three squadrons of Phantoms.[20] Some foreign defense experts in Seoul reportedly believe that from a purely military point of view, all United States ground forces could be withdrawn within two years without jeopardizing Seoul's defense.

The South Korean government is said to no longer fear an all-out attack by Kim Il Sung. Park himself is reported to have said that by 1981 South Korea will not need American ground forces to repel a North Korean invasion.

Certainly some changes in the current political and military situation on the Korean Peninsula can be anticipated in the next decade. However, changes should come slowly and with effective alternative guarantees for peace in this area.

Japan is particularly concerned by what happens in South Korea and would prefer that the United States keep its military strength at current levels. While reconciled to some reduction, Japan is pressing for prior consultation on any decision and for the United States to obtain prior assurances of noninterference before redeployment occurs.

Since the November election, President Carter has reaffirmed his campaign pledge to withdraw ground troops within five years but has indicated he will move cautiously, and this seems to have calmed the Japanese for the present.[21]

Twenty-eight years, 33,000 lives, $12 billion in foreign aid and America's foreign policy prestige have gone into the building of a prosperous non-Communist South Korea. Significant changes in what has been a successful policy could alter the power balance on the Peninsula, threaten Japan's security, reduce the credibility of the American commitment, and encourage Kim Il Sung to start a new war. Consequently the new administration should proceed carefully.

The allegations of corruption involving United States Congressmen, government officials, and the Korean CIA may quicken the attack of those to whom the Korean Government and its repressive policies on human rights are repugnant. Again, I would emphasize that the United States must not let these allegations sour our long-term security commitments toward the Republic of Korea, for what is involved here is an element of our total Asian defense policy, including the stability and well-being of Japan.

China.   In 1969 our government began taking steps designed to relax restrictions—limited to measures in the area of trade and travel—between the United States and the People's Republic of China (PRC). In 1971 Dr. Kissinger made two trips to China which paved the way for President Nixon's historic visit in February 1972. A joint communique issued in Shanghai at the end of that visit recognized that progress in the normalization of relations was in the interest of all countries, that international disputes should be settled without the threat or use of force, and that the development of trade between the United States and PRC should be facilitated.

President Ford, in his address to the joint session of Congress on April 10, 1975, reaffirmed United States support for the principles of the Shanghai Communique. President Carter has also indicated his support for normalizing relations with the PRC—establishing full diplomatic relations but without abandoning our obligations to the Republic of China. Accordingly, there is a broadly based desire in the United States to build on the progress made to date.

Liaison offices are now maintained in each other's capitals, visits of a cultural and commercial nature are increasing, and some trade is developing. The scope of this trade is limited by China's conservative trade and financial policies; foreign exchange reserves are modest; foreign indebtedness is eschewed; and imports tend to be scaled to export earnings. Also China does not receive most-favored nation tariff treatment in the United States market.

United States trade with the PRC rose to a two-way level of $923 million in 1974 but declined sharply in 1975—as is obvious from Table 4.9—and continued downward in 1976.

Table 4.9   United States Trade with Communist China
(millions of dollars)

YEAR	EXPORTS	IMPORTS
1972	$ 64	$ 33
1973	690	67
1974	807	116
1975	305	159
1976	150(e)	200(e)

SOURCE: Census Bureau, U.S. Department of Commerce.

(e) Estimate based on preliminary figures.

The prospects for future trade in raw materials, petroleum equipment, machinery, and high technology remain bright. Skeptics, on the other hand, say that "the potential market for United States products is limited to a few select product categories, that the purchases are non-recurrent, that the availability of a broad consumer market base may well be 40 to 50 years away, and that the emphasis is on self-sufficiency which exhibits itself in an interest in technology rather than products.[22]

Normalization of commercial relations and greater growth in trade is still impeded by a number of unresolved issues, such as normal banking and shipping relations, resolution of the linked issues of PRC assets blocked in the United States and United States private claims against China. Most-favored-nation tariff status and Eximbank credits can be granted to China only if a trade agreement is reached as required by the Trade Act of 1974; such an agreement involves a number of complex questions.

While mainland China with its 900 million people offers a promising long-term market, can the United States afford to disrupt its trade relations with the Republic of China which represents our second largest market in Asia? Our two-way trade with that country of 16 million people totalled $3.6 billion in 1975 and $4.8 billion in 1976, in fact many times the size of our trade with the mainland (see Table 4.10). United States investments in China (Taiwan) total $500 million and some 220 corporations with American investment, including eight United States branch banks, are operating on the island.

The question which needs resolution is how to achieve normalization of relations with mainland China without de-recognition of Taiwan. De-recognition involves important trade and investment issues. For example: Will Taiwan's exports to the United States be eligible for most-favored-nation treatment? For the special duty reductions under the general system of preferences? The question of insurance coverage for American investments on the island under the Overseas Private Investment Corporation (OPIC), which is a United States government institution, arises as well as the sale of nuclear fuels for Taiwan's power plants.

Table 4.10   United States Trade with China (Taiwan)
(millions of dollars)

YEAR	EXPORTS	IMPORTS
1972	$ 628	$1,293
1973	1,170	1,784
1974	1,427	2,098
1975	1,660	1,938
1976	1,800(e)	3,000(e)

SOURCE: Census Bureau, U.S. Department of Commerce.

(e) Estimate based on preliminary figures.

The United States has agreed to provide the island with nuclear fuels until 1995, but what will happen to that agreement if the Republic of China ceases to exist in the eyes of Washington? Although Premier Chiang Ching-kuo insists that his government is interested in only the peaceful uses of nuclear power, Peking cannot be expected to believe that and could try to pressure the United States into nullification of the nuclear fuels agreement.[23]

The legal status of American corporations is also a serious problem.

Certainly there are no easy solutions to the issues; the United States can only hope the new government in China might become so anxious for more normal relations as to permit us to extend recognition to Peking on the basis of its de facto control over the Chinese mainland and under a formula that recognizes one China and two governments. This formula would be opposed by both Peking and Taipei, but it appears to be the only realistic settlement at this time to a very complex problem.

Hong Kong. Any list of possible political developments likely to occur in East Asia in the next twenty-five years would be incomplete without mention of Hong Kong. This British Crown colony today consists of the two large islands of Hong Kong and Lan Tao, a portion of the mainland, and more than 200 smaller islands. The land area totals 398.5 square miles.

Hong Kong Island was granted to the British in perpetuity in 1842; in 1860, 3.5 square miles of the mainland comprising Stonecutters Island and Kowloon south of Boundary Street was ceded outright to Britain. The New Territories (365 square miles), including Lan Tao Island, became part of modern Hong Kong in 1898 under terms of a ninety-nine year lease. In the absence of unforeseen developments the lease will expire June 30, 1997.

Even now potential Western investors are raising questions—particularly in regard to large investments in the New Territories—where the rate of return may be small and protracted, depending on what political control will prevail beyond 1997. To date, the British and Peking governments seem to be taking the position that it is still too early to discuss the matter.

While the status quo may be good enough for the present, when the 1980s come to pass, mainland China's intention as regard both Hong Kong Island and the New Territories will become of great political and economic urgency. In this connection a Chinese letter of March 8, 1972, to the Chairman of the United Nations General Assembly's Special Committee on Decolonization defined Hong Kong as a "part of Chinese territory occupied by the British . . . authorities" and reserved China's right to settle the question "in an appropriate way when conditions are ripe."[24] No territorial limit was placed on China's reference to Hong Kong.

Trust Territory of the Pacific Islands.   This United Nations Trust Territory consists of ninety-seven inhabited atolls and separate islands of which the Mariana, Marshall, and Caroline Islands are the major groups. The territory has approximately 110,000 people and a combined land area of 700 square miles. It is administered by the United States.

On March 24, 1976, President Ford signed the Northern Mariana Commonwealth Covenant (Public Law 94-241) which will eventually bring the fourteen islands comprising the Northern Marianas into political union with the United States as a commonwealth. The population on these islands totals about 15,000 and the land area affected is 181.9 square miles. The political status of the inhabitants of the Northern Marianas will closely resemble that of neighboring Guam, a United States territory. On the basis of present plans, this new political relationship will become effective by the end of 1981 when the Trusteeship agreement is terminated for these islands.

The inhabitants of the Carolines and Marshalls have been negotiating with the United States for a number of years on a somewhat different basis referred to as a Compact of Free Association; the most recent negotiating session occurred June 2, 1976. As in the case of the Northern Marianas, the negotiators are endeavoring to develop a political framework which will enable these island groups to enjoy a large measure of self-government by 1981 when the Trusteeship is terminated. A definitive agreement does not seem far away.

SUMMARY

The land areas of East Asia and Oceania plus the Pacific Ocean cover approximately 40 percent of the earth's surface; nearly the same percentage of the world's population resides in this region.

While the largest part of this population is controlled by Communist regimes, the United States maintains relations with most governments in this area, enjoys healthy trade relations with many, and is contributing substantially to their economic development.

The countries with which this study is concerned are inhabited by intelligent, industrious people; they are blessed with substantial resources. Many of them are well along on programs for achieving economic viability. However, among the developed and developing free economies of East Asia there is a high degree of interdependence in regards to investments, accessibility of markets, and terms of trade. Two of the world's three largest industrial powers—Japan and the United States—are very intimately linked in their economic prosperity and growth and will be throughout the next quarter century. Both the United States and Japan experienced a turndown in domestic business activity during 1974 and 1975. However, recently both have installed new political leaders. Fortunately they recognize that new programs must be found to stimulate their national economies. The policies which they adopt will have great bearing on the ability of the free economies in this region to sell the output of their farms, mines, and factories to Japan and the United States. Expanded trade opportunities could greatly ease immediate and pressing economic and financial problems.

The United States enters the last quarter of this century with a security and trading system which has worked well. Our present position has been secured at great sacrifice—nearly one-half million casualties and heavy military expenditures and economic aid that reaches tens of billions of dollars. While political and economic adjustments will need to be made in response to changing circumstances, the present system should be maintained and strengthened.

Our friends in Asia are legion and should never again be disappointed—as so many were by our recent failure in Indochina. One, in particular, comes to mind whom we left in Cambodia.

As Ambassador John Dean planned his departure from Phnom Penh on April 12, 1975, he offered a seat to Sirik Matak, one-time prime minister under Lon Nol, in the last United States' military helicopter taking Embassy staff and others from Cambodia. The following reply is reported to have been received:

> "Dear Excellency and Friend: I thank you sincerely for your letter and your offer to transport me to freedom. I cannot, alas, leave in such a cowardly fashion. As for you, and in particular your great country, I never believed for a moment that you would have the sentiment of abandoning a people which have chosen liberty . . . I have only committed the mistake of believing in Americans. Please accept, Excellency, my dear friend, my faithful and friendly sentiments."

After the Khmer Rouge entered Phnom Penh, Sirik Matak was shot. Few Cambodians escaped.[25]

Let us make certain these nightmares of the immediate past are not repeated.

NOTES

[1.] *Washington Post*, 19 December 1976.

[2.] United States Overseas Loans and Grants: Obligations and Loan Authorizations, July 1, 1945-June 30, 1975.

[3.] World Bank, *Annual Report 1976*, p. 36.

[4.] *Ibid.*, pp. 120-21.

[5.] A stable state is predicted after 2075. See *The Future of the World Economy*, United Nations, 1976, p. 10.

[6.] *Far Eastern Economic Review*, 20 August 1976, p. 43.

[7.] *Washington Post*, 11 December 1976.

[8.] *Far Eastern Economic Review*, 20 August 1976, p. 44.

[9.] *Washington Post*, 1 December 1976.

[10.] Introduction and Summary, *The Future of the World Economy*, United Nations, 1976, p. 14.

[11.] *Washington Post*, 2 January 1977.

[12.] Recent reports indicate that China may not become the Saudi Arabia of the Far East and that forecasts that China would be exporting 350 to 700 million barrels of oil a year by 1980 are no longer thought valid. Production levels at China's richest and best-known oil field in Taiching in northeast China seemed to have peaked and are tending downward. *Washington Post*, 19 December 1976.

[13.] Address of Secretary of State Kissinger, Nairobi, Kenya, 6 May 1976.

[14.] *Ibid.*

[15.] *Washington Post*, 19 December 1976.

[16.] Remarks, Deputy Secretary of State Charles W. Robinson before the Conference Board in New York City, 16 September 1976.

[17.] *Far Eastern Economic Review*, 8 October 1976.

[18.] *Washington Post*, 28 December 1976.

19. *Washington Post,* 22 November 1976.
20. *Washington Post,* 13 November 1976.
21. *Washington Post,* 28 December 1976.
22. *Far Eastern Economic Review,* 10 September 1976.
23. *Ibid.*
24. *Far Eastern Economic Review,* 10 December 1976.
25. *Washington Post,* 2 January 1977.

FIVE

World Energy Needs 1977-1999

James Milton Voss

James Milton Voss, Chairman of Caltex Petroleum Corporation, has been associated with Caltex for more than thirty years. Much of this time was spent in China, Hong Kong, Japan, and Australia.

Joining Caltex in 1946, Mr. Voss was stationed in Shanghai for what proved to be a most eventful three years since he visited nearly every province of the country. During one anxious period, Mr. Voss was held for ransom by Communist-led students of Chaotung University and was released only after Mayor K. C. Wu, later governor of Formosa, interceded for him.

He was appointed Shareholders' Representative for Japan operations in 1956 and in 1960, Managing Director of Caltex Oil (Australia) Pty. Ltd. Late in 1961, he was recalled to New York as a Divisional Vice-President of Caltex; in May 1964 he was elected President. He became Chairman of the Board and Chief Executive Officer in 1970.

I have been asked to discuss the prospects for meeting world energy needs to the year 2000—a long time away for the young, but the day after tomorrow for those somewhat longer-in-the-tooth.

Meeting the world's energy needs raises immediately the question of just what they will be. Later, I will present a supply-demand forecast, fully conscious that two decades from now the data may be difficult to check or swamped by history and forgotten. Such are the "comforts" of the forecaster. Another "comfort" is that the forecast is the work of many people: it differs in degree from what several prominent experts are saying. But it is based on what we consider to be the best data and most supportable assumptions. In preparing the forecast, the works of the leading oil-economic seers and Caltex specialists here and abroad have been consulted, and some thoughts of my own have been added.

LOW COST ENERGY

Abundant and cheap energy supplies have been taken almost for granted during the world's evolution into its present industrial age. The limits of wood fuel and wind power were reached early in the nineteenth century and man then began to turn to fossil fuels such as coal and lignite. At the turn of this century, these fuels were still the main sources of the low-cost energy that had made possible the industrial revolution of the previous three quarters of a century. In time, hydroelectric power became a contributing source in areas blessed with waterfalls. Oil slowly entered the energy scene in the last two decades of the nineteenth century and assumed its present dominance only in the second half of this century.

Today, we approach depletion of all known reserves of oil and natural gas. Still, the public thinks of oil when it thinks of energy. Our automobiles, trucks, tractors, buses, ships, and airplanes run on it. And well they might because oil, and only oil, until recently has been capable of filling the ever-widening gap between total demand and the limited availability of other energy sources. But the age of cheap oil, and indeed of cheap energy, has gone. The economic law of supply and demand no longer controls the world pricing of oil. Political power and influence now dominates. The domination is largely through OPEC, the Organization of Petroleum Exporting Countries, which controls the major sources of crude oil. OPEC has rather arbitrarily set the world price of crude at eight to nine times what it used to be as recently as 1970.

The production costs of alternative sources of energy are generally known to economists and, hopefully, to governments. They should also know that oil prices must in the long term relate to these costs. But the long term may be a long time in coming. Meanwhile, a surplus — albeit temporary — of crude oil exists in the world, and economic theory would indicate that prices should relate to the cost of marginal production and fall drastically. But they haven't and won't, and it is precisely OPEC's political clout which has caused this.

ALTERNATIVE SOURCES OF ENERGY

Unfortunately, alternative sources of energy do not today hold the promise for us they once seemed to have.

As late as 1966, there were expert forecasts that nuclear plants would supply almost limitless sources of power. The atom was expected to provide the world's cheapest energy. But as of today, nuclear power is the sick man of industry. What happened?

Environmentalists attack it; its costs escalate. The world may run out of fissionable uranium before it runs out of oil. All known reserves of lowest-cost uranium will be committed by about 1981.

Breeder reactors, once highly regarded because they create plutonium for use from their own fuel, are so expensive that they may never be economically feasible. There is loud and resourceful opposition to nuclear power because its radioactive by-products—including plutonium—are viewed as threats to public health and safety.

The United States now has about sixty conventional nuclear reactors in operation. The nuclear power industry expects the number to approach 200 by 1985. By 2000, it is expected that 600 will be needed—over ten times what we have now.

Our forecast predicts that nuclear power will supply 14 percent of the nation's energy in 2000, up from 3 percent today. No significant contribution from breeder reactors is expected by then, however.

Nuclear fission processes which I have been discussing are not clean. But nuclear fusion might be. Ten years ago fusion, which merges rather than separates atoms, was hailed as the ultimate energy source, because its fuel, hydrogen, is abundant. Apart from unknown costs, this process has a very basic problem: no one yet knows how to build a fusion reactor.

Some predict the world will develop an economy based on the use of hydrogen. As a fuel, hydrogen is nonpolluting because it releases water rather than carbon dioxide when burned. But it is highly flammable when mixed with air and if placed in public use, especially in automobiles, could turn a minor collision into a major disaster. Further, its production on a major scale—by electrolysis or thermo-chemical processes—could result in a net increase in world energy consumption.

Methyl alcohol, commonly called methanol, has been successfully used as an automotive fuel component. But it is more expensive to pro-duce methanol from coal than to convert coal into other fuels, such as methane. And to go from methane, which is a natural gas, to methanol would result in another net energy loss to the world.

Still, research is dealing with the possible production of methanol from solid wastes, of which we have an oversupply. If the effort suc-ceeds, methanol could find a place in the energy family.

Solar Energy

There is one eternal energy source that scientists and environ-mentalists agree on as the ideal: the sun. While they agree on the desirability and the infinite possibilities of solar energy, experts differ widely on its applications and on the capital costs that will be required to create a solar energy system. I cannot offer you a consensus or a conclusion since neither has been reached. I can only tell you that while some are convinced that no one now alive will live in a solar energy world, others retort that the introduction of solar energy—es-pecially in the form of local heating applications—is already at hand. They contend that it can be cheaper than electric and other types of heating if one recognizes fully the real costs for the alternate energy supplies. Moreover, they say that even in the least favorable parts of the continental United States, there is sufficient sunlight to heat—and even cool—typical buildings without supplement. One claim is that if in the next twelve years we were to construct all new buildings with passive solar collectors—large south windows, or glass-covered black south walls—we would save as much energy as we expect to collect from the Alaskan North Slope. Work on solar heating and cooling is now being conducted by such firms as Honeywell, Owens-Illinois, N. V. Philips, Pittsburgh Plate Glass, and Revere. Among the major oil companies also engaged in this work are Shell, Mobil, and Standard Oil Company of California.

Geothermal Energy

Another nonconventional source is the volcanic heat of the earth, geothermal energy. Today, electricity is being produced by this technology in Italy, Japan, New Zealand, and the United States. Costs are within the range of five to eight mills per kilowatt hour. But known reserves are small; we have limited knowledge of the geology of these reservoirs or of their heat extraction capacities and allowable rates of cooling. One question to be resolved in the future is whether or not possible earthquake conditions will be created as heat is removed and the internal structure of the earth shrinks.

Processes are planned to extract oil and gas from oil shale. All are expensive, and most introduce serious environmental problems.

Some futuristic approaches include the use of laser beams in controlled fusion of hydrogen nuclei, harnessing of ocean tides and wind and wave action, and on-site gasification of underground coal deposits to avoid the high costs and environmental problems of mining.

As I indicated earlier, there is much more to the future energy picture than resource depletion and scientific solutions. Most important are the international politico-economic effects.

OPEC

A fact of global life is that, no matter where your sympathies lie in the complex war-peace-insurrectionary turbulence of the Middle East, OPEC has distinct political biases, and it controls the major sources of crude oil as well as the setting of world prices. Its members are, in the Arabian Gulf area: Iraq, Iran, Kuwait, Saudi Arabia, Qatar, and the United Arab Emirates; in Africa: Algeria, Libya, Gabon, and Nigeria belong. In Southeast Asia, there is Indonesia, and in the Western Hemisphere, Ecuador and Venezuela. This group is not politically monolithic—far from it. Through three Arab wars, Iran sent oil to Israel. Iran supported Kurdish rebels in Iraq for many years. Little admiration exists between the hereditary rulers of the Arabian Gulf and the doctrinaire thinkers of Algiers, Baghdad, and Tripoli. Indonesia to the east and Venezuela to the west are geographically and culturally far, far from their Middle Eastern partners.

The OPEC countries have their offstage wrangles, but they have always agreed on one thing: the price of crude should go up and should always keep pace with the world price of other goods. Until recently, they even agreed fully on the extent of each price rise. In 1970, the so-called "marker" crude, 34-degree Arabian Light, sold for as little as $1.35 a barrel. Today, it sells for over $12.00 a barrel—more than an eight-fold increase. It is a fact of your lives, just as it is of mine, that the OPEC countries—despite occasional disagreements among themselves—are in control of world prices.

How long will this last? There have been estimates, predictions, and prayers that OPEC will break up. Some say its weakness is excess capacity, that high prices, government-induced conservation measures, and new discoveries—such as the North Sea and Alaska—will require OPEC to enforce strict production schedules to avoid a world glut, and that its members will then start to cut prices in order to expand their shares of shrinking markets. The pricing divergence which emerged from the Qatar meetings last December—with Saudi Arabia and the United Arab Emirates opting for a 5 percent increase versus 10 percent for the rest—seems to support this line of reasoning. This is, of course, a fascinating development but it is too early yet to evaluate its true meaning as regards the future of OPEC. For myself, I wouldn't bet that it points to an early breakup of OPEC. For OPEC to be restrained at all, a viable counterforce must be developed by consuming nations.

The North Sea and Alaska reserves combined are nothing compared with Arabia alone. The only real forces that can be counted on ultimately to weaken OPEC are conservation combined with mass development of new energy sources. As we have seen, the latter are still up in the air. My assumption, therefore, is that OPEC will be with us indefinitely. This is the new reality.

CONSERVATION

Conservation, whether or not it helps to weaken OPEC, is a most important goal in itself. As is abundantly clear, the United States is a profligate user of energy and much of this is used most inefficiently. To a lesser degree, the same holds true for the rest of the developed world. Opportunities abound, therefore, for achieving significant energy savings without seriously affecting our economies or our life-styles. These would include better insulation of buildings, lighter and more efficient—i.e., better-mileage automobiles, and the cogeneration of heat and electric power in industry. Even capital costs favor conservation since generally the costs to save energy are far less than the costs of equivalent new energy.

What then does it take to make a concerted effort for conservation? There are institutional barriers—outmoded building codes, resistance from labor to concentrate in new areas, new value relationships needed on the part of the general public—but these surely can be broken through. What really needs to happen is for industry and the public at large to become aware of the true overall costs of energy. This could be done through elimination of price controls and other subsidies which continue to deceive the public into thinking that energy is still abundant and cheap. Only then will we develop our true potential for the efficient use of the energy we now have and for development of our underutilized resources. The economic savings represented by such developments would be a great boon not only to the world's economy but also to its ultimate ecological ability to sustain life as we know it on this planet.

LONG-TERM FORECAST

Now we come to what a New England Yankee would call the *heft* of my presentation—the forecast. Many long-term forecasts of energy demand and supply have been made recently—some for the U.S., some for the world. They have been made by oil companies, banks, public utility associations, and by agencies of the federal government. What is surprising is that they mostly agree that from 1985 to 2000 annual growth rates of total energy demand will be from 2.5 to 3.3 percent per year for the U.S. To me this implies that all economic planners know each other and have frequent discussions—and that there has been some high intensity crossbreeding in the production of these ostensibly independent forecasts.

Of them all, the Federal Energy Administration's forecast is by far the most comprehensive and sophisticated. It uses advanced techniques in mathematical modeling and computer programming applied to a tangle of economic data. However, it does not follow that the resulting forecast is necessarily better than others made with much less expenditure of time and money. This is because unrealistic assumptions throw up unrealistic results. For example, the FEA forecast favors $13 a barrel as OPEC's price for Arabian Light crude, delivered in New York, to apply through 1985. In fact, this price has already been exceeded, and with eight years to go.

Caltex Forecast

Our forecast differs from most of the others in detailing how a supply-demand balance will be achieved, in specifying key assumptions and problems, and in assessing the role of business.

This was the basic approach in developing the forecast: First, we boldly assumed a reasonable business climate for the next quarter century. We then analyzed world energy and economic trends for the past fifteen years and developed what we consider to be supportable correlations of Real Gross National Product and energy demand by end use.

Because exponential growth at any significant rate cannot go on forever, we assumed that the growth of the world economy must be at gradually decreasing rates. This should average 3.6 percent a year to the year 2000, which is roughly three quarters of the past long-term rate.

We then derived an initial demand forecast for each energy form from the foregoing assumptions and historical correlations.

The forecast was next adjusted for expected constraints such as capital shortages, OPEC price rises, mandated efficiencies in new cars, ceilings on world crude production, and for nuclear power plant construction. We think the resulting forecast represents a reasonable and attainable balance between demand and supply despite these constraints, many of which may turn out to be quite monumental.

The principal results are shown on Table 5.1 which compares the world's energy utilization in 1974—the last year for which complete data are available—with our forecasts for the year 2000.

Overall, the forecast indicates that world energy demand will grow to the end of this century at a decreasing rate, but averaging 3.6 percent per year for the period as demonstrated by Table 5.2. This is slightly under the 3.7 percent rate predicted for the economy as a whole. The difference is attributed to savings from conservation and

**Table 5.1   The World's Primary Energy Requirements
(as millions of BPCD of oil*)**

1974 ACTUAL	COAL	OIL	GAS	NUCLEAR	HYDRO/GEO	TOTAL
U.S.A.	6.4	16.6	10.5	0.6	1.4	35.5
Europe	5.1	14.0	2.9	0.5	1.7	24.2
Japan	1.1	5.6	0.1	0.1	0.4	7.3
Other OECD	0.9	2.5	0.9	0.1	1.1	5.5
Total OECD	13.5	38.7	14.4	1.3	4.6	72.5
Other Free World	2.7	8.8	1.6	—	1.2	14.3
Total Free World	16.2	47.5	16.0	1.3	5.8	86.8
Sino-Soviet	18.0	9.9	5.4	0.1	1.0	34.4
Total World	34.2	57.4	21.4	1.4	6.8	121.2
2000 Forecast						
USA	20.1	28.2	9.0	9.8	3.4	70.5
Europe	7.4	29.1	10.0	6.2	2.4	55.1
Japan	2.6	11.6	0.8	2.3	0.6	17.9
Other OECD	2.0	5.8	1.8	1.2	2.4	13.2
Total OECD	32.1	74.7	21.6	19.5	8.8	156.7
Other Free World	10.3	19.7	6.1	1.6	3.3	41.0
Total Free World	42.4	94.4	27.7	21.1	12.1	197.7
Sino-Soviet	38.6	31.3	20.9	8.4	5.2	104.4
Total World	81.0	125.7	48.6	29.5	17.3	302.1

SOURCE: Caltex.

*Barrels per calendar day.

more efficient utilization of energy in future years. For the United States alone, we predict an average growth rate of somewhat less, at 2.7 percent per year.

These figures imply that the doubling of world energy demand of the past fifteen years will require about twenty years at the forecasted lower growth rate.

Developed countries will continue to require more than 80 percent of the free world's energy needs and more than 70 percent of total world needs. The U.S. will account for about 23 percent of world requirements.

Table 5.2　Annual Growth Rates of World's Primary Energy Requirements

(% per year)

1960-1974 ACTUAL	COAL	OIL	GAS	NUCLEAR	HYDRO/GEO	TOTAL	RGNP
U.S.A.	2.5	3.8	4.2	—	5.1	3.9	3.8
Europe	(2.3)	9.4	21.0	—	3.2	4.9	4.6
Japan	2.3	17.3	—	—	2.1	11.0	9.8
Other OECD	2.9	6.0	11.3	—	5.8	6.1	5.0
Total OECD	0.3	6.8	6.1	—	4.2	4.9	4.8
Other Free World	2.9	6.8	12.7	—	10.4	6.5	5.4
Total Free World	0.6	6.8	6.5	—	5.1	5.1	4.8
Sino-Soviet	3.1	8.9	10.7	—	9.0	5.4	4.6
Total World	1.8	7.1	7.4	—	5.6	5.2	4.8
1974-2000 Forecast							
U.S.A.	4.5	2.1	(0.3)	11.3	3.5	2.7	3.4
Europe	1.4	2.9	4.9	10.2	1.3	3.2	3.5
Japan	3.4	2.8	8.3	12.8	1.6	3.5	4.5
Other OECD	3.1	3.3	2.7	10.0	3.0	3.4	3.4
Total OECD	3.4	2.6	1.6	11.0	2.5	3.0	3.6
Other Free World	5.3	3.2	5.3	—	4.0	4.1	4.0
Total Free World	3.8	2.7	2.1	11.3	2.9	3.2	3.7
Sino-Soviet	3.0	4.5	5.3	18.6	6.2	4.4	3.7
TOTAL WORLD	3.4	3.1	3.7	12.8	3.6	3.6	3.7

SOURCE: Caltex.

Oil will continue to dominate the energy scene, supplying almost half of the requirements of the free world. However, the share of total energy supplied by oil and gas will drop by about 10 percent, essentially offset by a corresponding increase in share for nuclear power. Coal will tend to hold its share at about 20 percent.

This country will shift away even more from gas and oil; as noted, we will show a slower rate of energy growth than the rest of the world. The energy share supplied by oil and gas in the U.S. will drop by more than 20 percent to roughly half of total supplies, offset almost equally by increases in the shares for coal and nuclear power. Absolute volumes of gas supplies will actually drop.

For Japan, the extremely high rates of growth for the economy and energy of the past—10 to 11 percent a year—will be more than halved but will remain somewhat higher than that of the rest of the world. This downturn is primarily traceable to the end of the era of cheap energy in January 1974. Japan, with all but one-fifth of its energy from costly imported oil, has had to revise its economic game plan to accommodate this change into a workable balance for its world trade. Clearly, Japan must increase the price and volume of its exports to pay its new oil bill and, just as clearly, Japan's nonoil trading partners must impose limits on such increases or suffer massive trade deficits of their own.

END OF OIL'S DOMINANCE

This clear dominance for oil to the end of this century will not extend very far into the next, because the end is really in sight for the oil era. The consensus is that the roughly 90 million barrels per calendar day of oil supplies needed to balance free world demand in the year 2000 will not be easily supplied because the requirements will exceed expected crude production. Any deficits must be made up from oils derived from shale, tar sands, and coal or other exotic sources, most of which are now rated at least twice as costly as conventional crude oils.

The dominance of oil in our look at things to come implies a continuation of current international oil movements, but on a larger scale. In most of the remaining years to 2000, this country will import about half its oil needs, increasingly from Arab sources. The rest of the developed countries of the free world will also rely increasingly on imports to meet their needs, with Japan most dependent. Western Europe will be next, requiring about 80 percent from imports despite North Sea discoveries. The remaining countries will be relatively less dependent.

The use of coal will accelerate, especially in this country, starting in the mid-1980s when OPEC should be in its strongest position to exact even higher prices. Existing and new technology to gasify and liquify coal will come off the back burner as a result of the escalating oil prices. This strategy will make economic sense for the long term, especially in this country with its 200 to 300 years of coal reserves.

Increased needs for electric power will be met in large part from new nuclear power plants built mainly in the developed countries of the free world. Greater utilization of nuclear power than that assumed in this forecast (11.3 percent annual growth for the free world) will be difficult to realize in the light of known constraints in the construction of these plants. As a result, the major part of the free world's increased needs for electric power will still have to be met from fossil fuels: coal in the U.S., mostly oil elsewhere. This scenario will pertain even though the growth of electricity demand will drop sharply from about 7 to 4 percent annually, but will remain above the 3 percent annual growth of total energy demand.

As a result, the dissipation of energy in processes of energy conversion, mostly to versatile but expensive electricity, will rise to roughly 30 percent of energy supplies because these processes are relatively wasteful. Energy then available for final consumption in the free world will be split three ways, roughly in equal parts to use by the industrial, transportation, and domestic-commercial-agriculture sectors. Oil use will continue to monopolize the transportation sector, with the continued dominance of gasoline, diesel, and turbine engines more or less of existing design and with no significant penetration of the vehicle population by battery-powered cars.

The U.S. will continue to account for half of the energy consumed in the transportation sector of the free world as a result of its physical size, relatively low prices, and the vehicular mobility within the country for economic and recreational ends. Despite increasing costs, the domestic and commercial sectors will accelerate the use of electricity for space and water heating, especially in the U.S. because of diminishing supplies of natural gas.

The pitfalls facing this forecast have been assessed to the extent possible. The biggest snag is to divine the impact of OPEC on oil supply and pricing. Equally important is the question of capital availability in an increasingly inflationary and capital-hungry world. Snags of somewhat lesser—but still considerable—magnitude stem from governmental policies. These are mainly supply constraints on business in this country in the form of proposals to dismember the oil industry vertically or horizontally, to continue price controls on oil and natural gas, to restrict the leasing of federal lands both on and offshore for energy development, and to impose excessive environmental restrictions which stifle supplies and escalate energy costs in fits of nostalgia for the pristine, sylvan environment of the American Indian's heyday on this continent.

VERTICAL DIVESTITURE

At this point let me digress to mention a single, present imponderable that can have an incalculable effect on the entire world of energy: that is the issue of divestiture of the major U.S. oil companies—to break them up into their component parts: producing, transportation, refining, and marketing.

A couple of years ago, few Americans had ever heard of divestiture, although divestiture bills had been coming before Congress for thirty years or more. But these proposals took on new life after the Organization of Petroleum Exporting Countries quadrupled the price in January 1974 and the oil companies were generally blamed for it. At that point, divestiture developed large followings in the Senate and the House.

Let me compress a little history: A chasm of disesteem exists between the left-of-center Washington politician and the multinational industrialist. Both have their reasons.

The politician regards the private executive as a stuffy technician who thinks government is business with the profit motive eliminated; who is sheltered from dissent; who speaks only to fellow executives, security analysts, and business schools; whose economic errors are shielded from the public; who chooses not to illuminate the mysteries of his vocation; and who knows not retribution.

The politician, often from a city area where dishonest policemen are called "businessmen," cannot believe that the practice of trade demands much intellect. He agrees with Dr. Samuel Johnson that, "Trade could not be managed by those who manage it if it were difficult." And so, Congress tends to pass mindless reforms that force an industry into a paralytic condition, then tells its managers they don't know how to do the job.

In turn the industrialist, sometimes with accuracy, sees the politician as a public liar; a perpetual candidate, captive of an inexperienced, ambitious staff; supporter of overregulating bureaucracies; and a hypocrite-egalitarian who suffers fools gladly. Further, Congressional indignation at shadowy overseas business payments disgusts him when he reads about the passing of cash in Washington and party girls on the payrolls of the righteous. The industrialist, too, can cite

Dr. Johnson, and—paraphrasing him—conclude that politics is the last refuge of a scoundrel. He gloomily foresees that Orwellian day when the regulators will outnumber the regulated.

Nowhere is this barrier of mistrust more ominous than in the confrontation between certain members of Congress and the international oil companies. The potential tragedy of divestiture is that it may one day be accomplished by legislators who know little about the oil industry and understand even less the ultimate effects of their actions.

Divestiture proponents say the oil companies are too big, as though that in itself were bad. The oil companies are big because they have to be. I will concede that petroleum is not a cottage industry. But you can't move 40,000,000 barrels a day in international commerce with a teaspoon.

Friends of divestiture say that if the oil companies were broken up into their component parts, each would still be a large company. What they do not perceive is that oil units are interdependent. All of them do not always make money. Also, size alone does not mean success: the Pennsylvania Railroad was a large company, as was the New York Central and the W. T. Grant Company. The Edsel Division of Ford had 15,800 employees, 1,200 dealers, and $400,000,000.

HORIZONTAL DIVESTITURE

I have spoken only of vertical divestiture. Horizontal divestiture is another threat. Such legislation would prevent oil companies from entering other branches of the energy business such as nuclear and coal. Horizontal divestiture would thus cut off the main supply of funds and knowledge for the development of new energy sources. On this I can only tell you that—depending on your age—your children or your grandchildren will live to see the end of the petroleum era. Petroleum is a nonreplenishable resource. Some day it will be gone. Thus, hasty enactment of horizontal divestiture legislation would be like preventing a livery stable operator in 1904 from planning ahead and installing a gasoline pump at the curb.

All of these constraints by government on business coupled with a combination of punitive taxes, investment disincentives, and trade barriers, such as the antiboycott measures directed against key oil supplying countries, will tend to siphon private capital away from the energy industry. This scenario may unfold during the next few decades when this industry will be hard put to scrape up the required massive investments—several trillion dollars in this country alone—to finance the additional facilities needed. This will be difficult even under an ideal business climate.

OTHER KEY ASSUMPTIONS

Another problem encountered in preparing our forecast relates to the assumptions made on the impact of higher energy prices and of conservation measures to reduce energy demand. To allow for this we assumed cutbacks in the order of 10-20 percent in energy demand from what might otherwise have been predicted for the year 2000. But these cutbacks may not come about for a number of reasons:

1. For example, the American public may insist on driving around in the largest available cars despite gasoline prices of $1 a gallon and higher;
2. Tenants of apartments may continue to waste heat so long as the landlord must foot the bill and rents are controlled; and
3. The economics of owning a one-family home in this country continue to dictate minimizing investment costs. This makes installing relatively wasteful electric heat with its high operating costs a viable energy option.

Yet another difficulty is the assumption that the comparatively favorable world weather conditions of the past several decades will continue for the next two or three. Serious forecasts by students of long-term weather trends indicate that we may be on the brink of another ice age, possibly starting by the year 2000, and with significantly colder winters occurring even sooner. If so, our forecast will require a substantial upward revision in energy needs, certainly in the space heating requirements of the domestic and commercial sectors of the developed countries.

The U.S. and other nations of the free world have formed the International Energy Agency, mainly to cope with the supply problems of another oil embargo and to develop and use new energy forms, especially solar. Our Energy Resources and Development Administration

(ERDA) cooperates with other developed countries on research projects dealing with new energy forms, such as coal liquefaction and gasification, solar energy, and magnetohydrodynamics, as well as projects for energy conservation.

The U.S. and Japan are going ahead with an Energy Research and Development Agreement which will include energy conservation as a key item for research in the long term. The private sectors of the two countries are proceeding along similar lines, especially in the area of coal liquefaction.

The impact of all this R&D effort on the world's energy balance over the next several decades is difficult to measure. The effort is not a small one. For example, ERDA alone will spend well over $2 billion annually over the next several years on its R&D, more than the current investment outlays of all but two of the largest oil companies in the world. So much money and effort is bound to yield meaningful results.

For this forecast, the impact of this R&D effort was assumed to be mainly in the direction of increased production of synthetic gas and oil from coal, tar sands, and shale oil. The resulting effect has been significant, yielding an increase of several percent in the contribution from these sources to the world's energy by the year 2000. However, an even larger impact from this effort is most likely to take place in the next century because of the long lead time required once a new process has been proven to be commercially viable.

ROLES OF BUSINESS AND GOVERNMENT

In conclusion, I would like to say a few words on what I take to be, perhaps too hopefully, the respective roles of business and government in providing a proper climate to meet the world's needs for energy.

The role of the business community must be more assertive and positive than it has been in dealing with the energy problem. Business should continue its basic job of competitively supplying energy from initial source to point of sale as efficiently as possible within reasonable environmental constraints.

But this will not be enough, especially in this country, where the oil business is usually pointed out as the villain of our country's energy ills. Unfair attacks and outright lies should be rebutted at once. The survival of the industry as now constituted depends on being more assertive on the issue of divestiture and the other fundamental energy issues, including price controls and excessive environmental constraints.

For its part, the government should look to what is best for our country in the long term in its handling of the energy problem. First, it should adopt a less adversary posture to the business community which, after all, will be handling the job of supplying energy.

The government should shore up rather than break up the oil companies. Short-term political gains deriving from price controls on oil and gas should be rejected to insure increased, competitive supplies in the long term of high cost oil and gas from our own sources, rather than from even higher cost foreign sources.

Second, our government should deal in foreign affairs on the basis of what is realistically in our country's self-interest.

We Americans could learn a great deal from our Japanese friends on the proper role of government and business. Over the years, I have observed and dealt closely with them. In Japan, business and government work together in relative harmony on common, important problems such as energy. A consensus on a desired course of action is agreed to after intensive study and discussion at all working levels. Thereafter, the Japanese are unswerving in their dedication to carry out what has been agreed to. Thus, Japan in order to survive economically—while lacking our wealth of natural resources—cannot afford the social and political infighting that typifies our approach to resolving many pressing national problems, including energy supply.

To duplicate the Japanese approach is, I know, neither possible nor necessarily desirable in this country with its vastly different cultural heritage and economic situation. Nevertheless, some new approach to working in better harmony on the part of business and government should be possible. At least, this is the hope tacitly built into my outlook for the long-term business climate and the resulting forecast for meeting the world's energy needs.

SIX

International Business In Latin America:
An Overview of the Year 2000

William B. Wolf

Currently Professor of Industrial and Labor Relations at Cornell University, Dr. Wolf's experience in academia includes teaching positions at the University of Southern California, the University of Washington in Seattle, and the University of Chicago.

Dr. Wolf is one of the leaders in the field of business management. He served as President of the Academy of Management in 1971, and as Chairman of the International Management Division of the Academy of Management in 1973.

He is a prolific writer, having authored nine books and chapters in other books plus many articles.

Besides his academic work, he is a consultant to business and government agencies in the areas of management development, work simplification, organization design, human relations, et cetera.

The purpose of this paper is to make some educated predictions of the shape of things to come relative to international business in Latin America. At the outset, it must be recognized that this task is almost beyond mortal capability. The Latin Americas consist of twenty-one countries plus an assortment of Carribean Islands. Moreover, these countries vary from Mexico in the North to Chile and Argentina in the far South. Their governments range from democracies to dictatorships and their dictatorships vary from right wing to leftist. Most important, international business is not easily isolated from the rest of the world: it is an area where economics and politics come together and where the only safe generalization is that "everything is related to everything else."

The close interrelation between the various countries of the world is illustrated by recent events in the U.S. steel industry. Currently, the industry is seeking government protection from "cheap" foreign steel and from "unfair" trading practices by foreign producers. Critical problems arise because of the impact of steel upon the U.S. balance of payments. In one year, the United States imports approximately $4 billion in steel products. The current problem focuses upon Japan, Western Europe, and the U.S. The Japanese have agreed to limit exports to the European Common Market; this creates an excess of about 1.5 million tons of Japanese steel which will seek U.S. markets. To effect sales in the U.S., the Japanese have cut prices. Allegations have been made that the Japanese are dumping steel in the Gulf Coast markets and that they are artificially undervaluing the yen; this disrupts the U.S. markets. My point is simple: An agreement between the Japanese and the European Common Market has serious repercussions on the U.S. This, in turn, has repercussions upon all those countries with whom the U.S. trades. The manner in which the U.S. deals with the steel problem may unleash tension in many other areas of foreign trade. For example, President Ford established quotas on imports of special alloy steels from Japan and Europe; this could signal a return to protectionism and restriction in contrast with free trade. The point to be emphasized is that there is a significant economic interdependency between nations and with increased specialization and competition, this interdependency is increasing. Moreover, the implications are that a nation cannot readily stand alone. It is affected by events and happenings beyond its own borders. For example, if a financially weak country tries to expand its domestic economy, the result may be deterioration in its balance of payments, a collapse of its exchange rate, and enhanced inflationary pressures. Ultimately, the world must be viewed as an integrated system. It is specious to discuss or predict international business in a specific area without predicting for every other area. Thus, what is presented here is really an oversimplification and implicit in the presentation are many assumptions which should be rigorously spelled out. Unfortunately, due to limitations of time, space, and resources, many of these assumptions must remain implicit.

With the above caveat, I wish to consider the future of international business in Latin America. My point of view is that of the manager of international firms. The general goal is to stimulate thought which in turn may lead to constructive policy decisions.

THE WORLD ECONOMIC SYSTEM

The starting place for viewing the year 2000 is consideration of the global picture. By 2000, the world economic order will have been revised so that it is more rational and fair to developed and less developed countries (LDCs). The current chaos of floating exchange rates and movements toward restrictive trade practices will have been reversed. Some of the significant changes will be:

1. The General Agreement on Tariffs and Trade (GATT) will be totally renovated to promote free trade and a stronger program on commodities.
2. GATT will establish rules that protect and regulate multinational corporations (MNCs).
3. A new International Monetary Fund (IMF) will function like an "international" Federal Reserve System. It will be able to expand and contract the international money supply and will fix all foreign currency rates in terms of a new monetary unit (probably called Bancor).
4. The new IMF will also help national banks and MNCs if they are in trouble. It will be similar to "banker of last resort."
5. The World Bank (WB) will function differently; instead of raising funds on private capital markets, it will borrow Bancor from IMF. Thus, more financial aid will be available to LDCs.
6. GATT will be empowered to prevent discriminatory access and control of raw materials markets. Thus, export controls such as the OPEC embargo on oil shipments in 1973 will be outlawed.

The above are some of the more significant changes that we can expect by the year 2000. In essence, the world climate will have changed to recognize the interdependency of nations. There will be greater reliance on international institutions to deal with problems such as environmental issues, economic interdependence, and basic human needs. In short, new international institutions will be developed to provide a new economic and political climate in the world—a climate in which international business in Latin America will be significantly influenced: (1) rich nations will help LDCs to process their raw materials; (2) tariffs will be reduced on imports from LDCs; (3) economic aid to LDCs will be increased; (4) the heavy debt of LDCs will be rescheduled; (5) exchange variations will be such as to maintain par values.

These predictions are extremely optimistic and one might ask for some justification. The answer lies in the fact that they are drawn from the report of the Trilateral Commission composed of officers of the largest corporations in the Western world whose members come from Europe, North America, and Japan (the trilateral area). The report is an overall response to "the group of 77"—a group of third world nations who published a report in 1974 calling for a new international order.[1] Most important, the Trilateral Commission's report is probably the basis of the Carter administration's foreign policy; both President Jimmy Carter and Vice-President Walter Mondale were members of the Commission. Moreover, to date President Carter has appointed thirteen members of the Commission to government jobs including Cyrus R. Vance, the Secretary of State; Harold Brown, the Secretary of Defense; and W. Michael Blumenthal, the Secretary of the Treasury.[2]

Within the jurisdiction of the new economic system, there will be a code of conduct regulating MNCs and host nations which will deal with the major sources of conflict between MNCs and host countries. These include:

1. Transfer pricing and other accounting practices that shift profits to countries with lower rates of taxation will be halted;
2. Repatriation of capital and profits; standards will be set for reinvestment of earnings;
3. Full disclosure of MNC activities; MNCs will be required to make public complete descriptions of the activities of their principal affiliates in the world.
4. Full disclosure may also require reports on the number of nationals at various levels in the MNC, amount of local taxes paid, and percentage of materials from local sources.
5. Certain ethical practices will be identified; the code of conduct

for MNCs will include provisions prohibiting bribes, donations to political parties, or kickbacks.
6. Restrictive trade practices by MNCs will be outlawed, e.g., restrictive cartels and predatory competition will be prohibited.

The above are general changes in the nature of the world economic scene which will have impact upon Latin-American business. However, these changes in themselves will not guarantee prosperity or even reasonable growth. Other factors such as political stability, inflation, and market structures are of significant importance to the future.

POLITICAL STABILITY

Two kinds of political instability are visible in Latin America. First, there are the rivalries and antagonisms between nations. Secondly, there is the torment and friction which exists within the states themselves.

There is a long history of nationalistic rivalries in Latin America: it is almost the 100th anniversary of the Chilean burning of Lima, Peru; the Chaco war between Paraguay and Bolivia lasted five years (1933-38); and there have been numerous other territorial disputes. Even now there are serious border disputes such as Honduras versus Guatemala, Surinam versus Guyana, Venezuela versus Brazil, Venezuela versus Guyana, Colombia versus Venezuela, and Chile versus Argentina. These represent possible sources of friction and also a vulnerability to outside agitation. For example, as recently as June 1976, it was reported in a rightist Venezuelan newsweekly that there were three Cuban Communist military camps in Guyana. I should add that the *Time* magazine correspondent who investigated this accusation found no sign of such a Cuban occupying force. Currently Venezuela claims almost half of Guyana; the rich mineral resources of the area make it worth contesting.[3]

There is also strain between Chile and Peru. The Peruvians have been purchasing Russians armaments and have reinforced their border. Although these and other Latin-American rivalries are serious, they are not devastating and hardly compare with those found in Europe. Yet, they could escalate if contested territory is found to be blessed with rich deposits of natural resources such as tin, oil, or copper.

Also, the rivalries between the nations can conceivably be used to advantage if an outside nation wishes to agitate and stir up an ideological war. Such a possibility brings us to consideration of the internal political stability of the Latin-American nations. The situation resembles a powder keg that could explode at any time in the future; its fuse is the wide difference between the rich and the poor. In almost every Latin-American country, a small group of rich families, the military, or a small bureaucratic elite controls the country's economy.

The bulk of the population is poor and uneducated. Many of the countries have attempted to correct the situation: Peru, Chile, Mexico, and others have had land reforms to give the peasants land and to break up the holdings of the large haciendas. However, the success of these and other reform movements is not too significant. Moreover, the rate of population growth in Latin America is overwhelming. Estimates vary but they tend to agree that the population increase is from 3 to 3.5 percent per year. At that rate the population will more than double by the year 2000.

Yet, food production has not increased at a comparable rate. Already Mexico's population has increased to a level where its food supply is inadequate. By the year 2000, there may be severe food shortages in some Latin-American countries. I should also add that, in tune with my optimistic prediction about the world economic situation, I do not really expect a Malthusian dilemma by 2000. Rather, the Latin-American countries will begin to realize their true agricultural production potentials and become one of the main sources of the world's food supply. This is already evident in Brazil where the development of soybeans has resulted in that country becoming one of the world's major sources. In Brazil today, soybean exports exceed coffee in value.[4] Brazilian production of soybeans increased from 700,000 tons in 1968 to around 11 million tons in 1975. By 1980 it will probably be close to 20 million tons and by 1985 it should have surpassed the U.S. production of 30-40 million tons.

Still, the problems of rich versus poor and the explosive growth of population highlights the fact that internal dissension and stress exists in most Latin-American countries. With the exception of Venezuela, Mexico, and perhaps Colombia, the Dominican Republic, and Costa Rica, most of the governments are dictatorships—many of them are authoritarian and oppressive. In recent years there have been reports of tyranny and violations of basic human rights. The tradition of Latin America having "revolving door governments" is not exactly dead. There have been new governments in Argentina, Peru, Ecuador, and Chile in recent years.

To add to the turmoil, many Latin-American countries are currently battling terrorism and internal breakdowns caused by dissident groups: almost any American businessman in Argentina can tell you horror stories of what has happened to some executives of MNCs. The cost of the current revolution in Argentina is dazzling—as William Buckley stated—in Argentina in the past couple of years "more people have been executed by the terrorists and counter terrorists . . . than during the French Revolution."[5] The current problems of internal dissent go much beyond the Marxist ERP (Ejercito Revolutionario del Pueblo) and the Peronist-oriented Montonero (guerilla) movement. There are religious leaders who are exponents of the "theology of liberation" whose primary goals are liberation from dominance by outside economic interests and promotion of class struggles which could be interpreted as a religious support for guerilla activities. There are also numerous groups such as exiled Chileans, Cubans, and Guatemalans who are plotting revolt and contributing to political unrest.

To illustrate the potential instability within a Latin-American country we can examine Mexico. She is one of the major nations in Latin America. In the past two decades, Mexico has made remarkable strides in developing its industry and agriculture. Real growth averaged better than 7 percent through the 1960s, 6 percent in the early '70s (i.e., 1970-74); in the recession year of 1975, the real growth was approximately 4 percent. As evidenced by purchases of television sets, autos, and hot water heaters, the basic standard of living of many people had moved up. Mexico City, with 12 million residents, ranks as the world's third largest megalopolis. Mexico is self-sufficient in oil and has recently discovered vast new oil fields.

Yet, just a few months ago Mexico was on the verge of revolution. Many Mexicans were disgruntled with their one-party political system. They want a power of choice and discussion in political affairs. This coupled with inflation and pressures from the peasant groups urging more and faster land reforms, have caused concern as to whether the administration of newly elected President Portillo will survive. It should be added that the U.S. needs and wants a stable neighbor to the South; hence the Carter administration has already moved to support Lopez Portillo. But Mexico is currently facing serious problems. Unemployment is nearly 40 per cent; the foreign debt is about $25 billion; and the government must rely heavily upon the IMF (it has a $1.2 million credit) and the World Banking community. Most important, investor confidence must return.

Despite short-run crises such as Mexico's and despite all sorts of internal turmoil within Latin-American countries, I look toward increased stability and prosperity. One of the main reasons is that with increased material well-being, the degree of agitation will subside. And if the general world economic order is changed to recognize the global nature of national problems, then the gross distortions arising from intensive competition between nations will be mitigated.

INFLATION

A complicating factor in the future is inflation. Although international parity of currencies may be maintained, the currency of any specific country will still be vulnerable to depreciation. Inflation seems to be endemic to our world. Its history goes back to debasing coins during the time of the Crusades. Over the long run, every industrial nation appears to experience inflation. It is important to note that controlled, gradual inflation is not necessarily all evil: it eases the burden of debt, facilitates the transfer of resources from declining areas to expanding industries, and creates a psychological outlook of expansion and growth.

It appears that the year 2000 will find inflation continuing in most countries of the world. This will be especially true of Latin America and will be true despite pressures from the IMF, GATT, and WB for countries to apply deflationary measures. One force contributing to continued inflation is the level of national debt. The servicing and repayment of such huge debts becomes easier if there is a gradual, controlled inflation. In effect, the debt is repealed by inflation—cheap pesos or dollars, et cetera are used to repay the debts.[6] Moreover, a controlled inflation can contribute to an optimistic business outlook. Unless there is rampant inflation, people do not tend to think in terms of real income. By the year 2000, most nations in Latin America should have slowed their inflations to 6-10 per cent.[7]

REGIONAL INTEGRATION AND MARKET STRUCTURES

The Pan-American Cooperation ideal is as old as Simon Bolivar. In 1826, a conference was held in Lima where a declaration of the Principles of Solidarity of America was accepted by all twenty-one Latin-American Republics. Since this date several organizations have been formed to establish free trade and economic cooperation. In 1960, the Latin American Free Trade Association (LAFTA) was created. Also in 1960, the Central American Common Market (CACM) was established. The Andean Group was formed in 1969 and in that same year the River Platt Basin group was established. These efforts at establishing common external tariffs, regional industrial planning, and common rules to regulate foreign investors have met with only moderate success. For example, by the late 1960s LAFTA ran into problems related to the complexity of its negotiations, conflicts over objectives, and the imbalance between the volume of trade in different countries.

The Andean Pact (Ancom) was originally formed by Chile, Peru, Ecuador, and Colombia; in 1973 Venezuela joined. Ancom's goals are to knit together a full-scale industrial economy capable of dealing with MNCs and with competition from Brazil and industrial nations. It seeks to do this by promoting free trade among its members, allocating industrial production, and pooling capital and technology. To date its success is questionable. In November of 1976 Chile withdrew arguing that the restrictions on profit remittances by MNCs and Decision 24 which obligated foreign firms to "fade out" their control over the enterprises over a fifteen-year-period had discouraged foreign investment. Chile concluded that the continual absence of foreign capital implied that Andean Pact Nations had to achieve their desired growth rates primarily from local savings and decreased consumption. Furthermore, Chile argued that foreign investment is necessary to bring in technology and market know-how. Although Colombia and Venezuela still defend the Pact, both Peru and Ecuador—whose military regimes have changed and moved toward a more conservative stance—are applying pressure against the Pact's investment rules. In conclusion, regional integration in Latin America has had only moderate success. It appears that in the future the various nations will tend to develop their own markets and go their own ways. As *Business Latin America* suggests " . . . this would get away from the problem of having governments engage in production allotment poker games as they do now in both Ancom and LATA."[8]

Part of the pressure against regional integration will come from the changing structure of trade within Latin America. Venezuela, Mexico, Brazil, and Argentina already have industrialized enclaves. Their trade with Asia and Africa will increase in terms of manufactured goods as well as raw materials, e.g., MNCs with subsidiaries in Brazil report increasing trade with African nations. Angola has ordered $14 million worth of trucks from the Brazilian subsidiary of Sweden's SAAB SCANIA. In 1976, J. I. Case do Brasil sold approximately $2.5 million in excavating equipment to black Africa. And in 1976, Volkswagen do Brasil had sales to Nigeria of $28.5 million.[9] Government-controlled firms will also share in the growing export business: One illustration is the report that the Brazilian government's controlled-resource company, CIA, Vale do Rio Doce, S.A. recently signed long-term contracts to supply iron and pulp to Japan; the total value of the contracts exceeded $8 billion.[10]

By the year 2000 a number of the Latin-American countries will be exporting technology as well as primary goods and manufactured items. Already Mexico is exporting such know-how as the HYL direct-reduction process for manufacturing steel, developed by Mexico's largest private steel company. This has been sold to Venezuela and to Brazil.[11] Similarly, the Mexican Petroleum Institute's special oil refining process, DEMEX, has been sold to Jamaica and to Colombia's state oil company. The Cortina method for preassembling concrete structures is used in Saudi Arabia, Colombia, and Venezuela. Another Mexican development, the CUSI process for making newsprint from sugar bagasse, has been sold to Peru and Argentina. Thus, there are reasons to believe that nations which have been adapting technology from all over the world for their own purposes will eventually have their own know-how to sell. Moreover, in Latin America the common language and similarity of needs among nations tend to provide a natural economic trade bond. Overall, one can expect an increasing volume of trade, a changing mix (although Latin America will still deal mostly with primary products), and changing trade directions. With the developments suggested by the Trilateral Commission, trade will be more multilateral and bilateral trade agreements will decrease.[12]

The movement toward free trade, ownership restrictions on foreign firms, stable exchange rates, et cetera should significantly influence the volume of exports from Latin America. However, the region's balance of trade will probably continue to be negative and some of the countries will still need to restrain imports.

Attitudes toward Foreign Investments

Already there is a positive attitude toward foreign investment. Currently, a dominant theme in Latin America is to invite foreign capital: Argentina and Chile have liberalized their investment laws, returned expropriated firms, or provided compensation for seized assets. In these nations, private enterprise is looked upon as an important agent in economic growth. Even Peru has moved from a leftist dogma toward more pragmatic economics. In 1975 the Army commander-in-chief Francisco Morales Bermúdaz seized control of the country; to gain foreign backers and support he devalued the sol 31 percent and raised both prices and taxes. However, the government is still aiming at establishing "worker participation" in most industries.

Brazil previously had a policy to encourage foreign investment. In 1975-76 it reversed this and turned to restrictive trade practices and an import substitution policy. Since 1975, importers have had to deposit for 360 days with the nation's central bank a sum equal to the value of the imported goods. However, the recent appointment of Calmon de Sá as Minister of Industry and Commerce seems to indicate a more favorable attitude toward foreign investment.[13]

The attitude toward foreign investment is tempered by a continuing nationalism. Latin Americans want capital but they don't wish to give away control to their birthrights. Rather, they desire to attract foreign investment but not to lose independence and control. The dominant form of control is the joint venture with 51 percent ownership by nationals of the host country. The pattern for joint ventures varies from the Andean Pack's rules on "fade out" to the Peruvian system where workers, through profit sharing, eventually acquire 50 percent of ownership. Current evidence indicates that industries with high technology can obtain special treatment under joint venture laws; for example, IBM continues to be a sole proprietor in most of its overseas subsidiaries.

By the year 2000 the joint venture will dominate MNC holdings in South America. To deal with fears of foreign control, MNCs will staff predominantly with nationals of the host countries, move nationals into home offices, and give their companies a more international tone. Most subsidiaries in foreign countries will be dominated by the host nation's equity ownership.

A great future for MNCs in Latin America is technology transfer; by selling know-how, the MNCs will prosper. Such things as management development, inventory control systems, market research, organizational design, operating manuals, as well as technical processes and formulas, fall under the concept of technological transfer. Latin-American nations see knowledge as an important form of capital. They wish to import it, duplicate it, disseminate it, and make it available to their nationals. By the year 2000, it will be one of the significant areas of international business.

In summary, we can expect joint ventures to be the predominate form of MNC investment by the year 2000. Nationalism will remain—but perhaps be a little more flexible in its regulations. The service industries,—i.e., those selling technology—will be a major element in international trade.

The Overall Investment Climate

The theme of this forecast is almost self-evident. By the year 2000 the Latin-American countries will be one of the great areas for investment. They will be well on their way to full economic development, and they will be doing so through a reliance upon a mix of private investment and public corporations.

In terms of natural resources and agricultural potential, they will develop as major suppliers of the world's needs. This note of optimism is anchored on the prediction that we are about to see a new international economic system which will solve or mitigate many of the problems of world trade and give special support to LDCs. The one area this forecaster fails to come to grips with is the political stability within the various countries. Can dictators preserve political stability and promote economic progress for the next twenty-three years? True, Stroessner has been president of Paraguay for twenty-three years—but there is little evidence of economic progress there. In Brazil, Giesel alleges he is committed to eventually turning the government over to civilian rule. Chile is ruled by a right-wing military government. Argentina is ruled by a military president, Jorge Rafael Videla, and it appears that the military will remain a power for the next ten to fifteen years. However, currently there are rumors of dissent between the Army and Navy and General Videla over his position for dealing with civilian dissidents.[14]

What cannot be predicted is the amount of revenge, recrimination, and hate inspired by arbitrary, cruel acts of authoritarian leadership. Any visitor south of the border soon learns of the injustices perpetrated on the people (generally the political opposition). Arbitrary incarceration, torture, and murder have been associated with governments throughout Latin America. The turmoil triggered by injustice and violation of basic human rights may erupt at any time. In a trip through South America in 1973, I inadvertently was caught on the streets between police and rioters in Lima, arrived in Santiago after the general strike to support Allende had resulted in considerable destruction—and bullet holes in my hotel, and arrived in Buenos Aires the day after Peron's return (over 300 persons had been wounded and 33 killed at the airport). In Brazil I had drinks with a top man in industry—he was like a tea kettle with too much steam. He burst out about human freedom and his fear of "disappearing" for being outspoken and critical. Only in Venezuela did I feel secure. But there one of my hosts turned out to be a former S.S. officer who still believed in many of the worst practices of the Third Reich. Yes, the Achilles tendon of Latin America is the internal conflict, the values of many people which frequently emphasize power rather than achievement, and the deprived masses who live in abject poverty.[15] My hope is that increased reliance on private capital and market mechanisms will help disseminate positive values which combine the best of the Latin culture with those values essential to economic growth and development. In last analysis, at the heart of the future of business in Latin America are questions of the values of men and the philosophy of life; these I cannot be so presumptuous as to forecast.

NOTES

1. The Trilateral papers are available from the Trilateral Commission, Rm. 711, 345 E. 46th Street, New York, N.Y. 10017.

2. *The Christian Science Monitor,* Jeremiah Novak: "Report hints foreign policy shift," 14 February 1977, pp. 1, 6.

3. Cf. *Time* magazine, 7 June 1976.

4. *Business Week,* 18 October 1976, p. 112.

5. William F. Buckley in a syndicated column appearing in the *Ithaca Journal,* 2 February 1977.

6. Of course, this is an oversimplification and depends upon many fiscal and monetary practices but, as a general trend, it tends to hold.

7. It should be emphasized that the above prediction hinges on the success of the Trilateral Commission and its recommendations which will provide large supplies of capital for LDCs and encourage their development and processing of their commodities.

8. *Business Latin America,* 1977, p. 11.

9. *Business Week,* 1 November 1976, p. 39.

10. *Wall Street Journal,* 24 September 1976, p. 4.

11. This company, Hojalata y Lamine, developed the HYL process in collaboration with M. W. Kellog Co., Houston, Texas which is a subsidiary of Pullman Inc. For details see *Business Week,* 30 August 1976, p. 40.

12. These concepts of multilateral trade talks are stressed in the Latin American Commission's suggestion to the Carter Administration. The Commission on U.S.-Latin American Relations is a bipartisan group brought together by ex-OAS ambassador Sol Linowitz. See *Business Latin America* 174, p. 353; *Business Latin America* 176, pp. 313, 401.

13. See *Business Week,* 28 February 1977, p. 44.

14. See *The Christian Science Monitor,* 29 December 1976, p. 7.

15. For documentation of this see the work of David McClelland, especially his study of Venezuela.

SEVEN

International Tourism and Travel

David L. Edgell

David Edgell serves as Director of the Office of Policy Analysis of United States Travel Service (USTS), the U.S. Department of Commerce agency which is the national government tourism office.

In this capacity, he is responsible for all aspects of policy development for USTS including studies to identify the economic impact of proposed federal regulations and legislation on the tourist industry.

Edgell joined USTS in June 1976. He presently teaches graduate seminars in economics and policy analysis at George Washington University and is a frequent speaker before business, labor, and academic groups.

INTRODUCTION

The series of dynamic events that have occurred in the past few years in tourism and travel—and the likelihood of its optimistic growth potential for the future—merit and, indeed, require the focusing of attention on the significance of this commercial activity in

*Special recognition and credit for the preparation of this paper are due the following members of the Office of Policy Analysis, United States Travel Service: Jean G. O'Brien, senior policy analyst, and Stephen A. Wandner, senior economist, in the preparation of the text materials and Phyllis Jordan and Joyce Murphy in carrying out the administrative and clerical responsibilities. Valuable input was also received from the Division of Research and Analysis, United States Travel Service.

American economic and foreign policy.[1] The success of the tourism industry will depend heavily on the United States pragmatically exercising its responsibilty in planning public policy initiatives, coordinating policy with the private sector, and explaining to the public the important role tourism plays in international (and domestic) economic policies. In short, there is a real planning, coordination, and educational effort that needs to be accomplished if tourism is to take its proper place among the giants of American industry.

While international tourism to the United States has been discussed in many forums and approached from different avenues, it has suffered from inadequate planning and policy direction.[2] This paper will attempt to sift through the numerous facts and information on the subject and to look especially at its economic and foreign policy implications while at the same time broaching other important tourism issues. In the process, it will examine the prospects for international travel and tourism for the rest of the century.[3] It will explore the likely developments in this large and growing sector of the economy and attempt to suggest what these changes will mean to the United States. The focus through the "looking glass" will emphasize that international tourism in the U.S. has an optimistic growth future, if proper policy planning is forthcoming.

While the U.S. is a highly developed industrial nation relative to many European countries, it is somewhat underdeveloped with respect to international tourism. The European nations have recognized the essentiality of tourism to their economies and have approached its development and launched its programs with the same vigor the U.S. applied in putting a man on the moon. In the meantime, very little coordinated short-range or long-range planning by the government has taken place in this vital growth sector of the U.S. economy. Yet, if this country is: (1) to foster economic growth through increasing international tourism receipts, (2) to encourage tourism as a part of our foreign policy, and (3) to maintain our nation's natural beauty and other vital resources, planning is essential.

There are those among us who feel that the influx of tourists has the potential of destroying or injuring our natural and historical heritage. But if we look ahead for a moment, we can see both beneficial and unfortunate aspects of tourism with respect to the ecological balance and cultural inheritance of this country. With proper planning, reserves can be set aside in the form of national parks, seashores, and forests, both to protect finite scenic resources from overuse or exploitation and to increase travel opportunities for tourists. In addition, tourism, given its proper consideration in national priorities, can aid in maintaining our historical and cultural heritage, preserving and restoring traditions, while at the same time adding to the quality of life of those who wish to enjoy the benefits of such important social aspects of this great country.

Tourism will occur with or without planning; it is an essential part of life in today's world. Many people seek their release from tensions and strains of modern living in travel and tourism. People want a change of pace, an opportunity to experience life in new and different places. As the world prospers, this aspect of modern life—travel and tourism—will become a more important factor of U.S. economic and foreign policy, and it will have a major impact on environmental policy and land-use and other social values which add to the quality of life of society.[4]

This discussion is divided into four sections. First, international tourism as a commercial and economic activity is discussed. Second, the foreign policy and social aspects of international tourism are presented. Third, projections of tourism through the year 2000 and the implications of these projections are examined. And fourth, some conclusions and recommendations are considered.

INTERNATIONAL TOURISM AS A COMMERCIAL AND ECONOMIC ACTIVITY

Few are aware of the economic importance of tourism. For example, tourism generated $29 billion in world receipts in 1974 or roughly 6 percent of total world trade. By 1975, tourism receipts were $34 billion, an increase of 17 percent over 1974; in 1976 preliminary figures are that tourism receipts were $40 billion or almost 18 percent over 1975. Tourism constitutes one of the largest single items in world commerce and, in dollar terms, exceeds trade in iron and steel, ores and minerals.

International tourism to the U.S. is a large and rapidly growing sector of commercial activity. The United States share of total world tourism, however, is well below our national potential. Statistics for 1976 (the year of the U.S. Bicentennial) show that the United States hosted an estimated 17.5 million international visitors, an increase of 11.2 percent over 1975. An estimated 22.9 million Americans traveled abroad in 1976, down about 2 percent compared to 1975 departures. Preliminary data show U.S. receipts from international visitors totaled $6.8 billion in 1976, a notable 20 percent increase over 1975. Expenditures by Americans traveling abroad totaled $9.45 billion, a 7 percent increase from 1975. Tourism expenditures by foreign travelers in the U.S. have grown, on an average, by 8.2 percent per year in real terms since 1960—a much faster growth rate than real GNP during the same period. Even so, the U.S. share of total international travelers is less than 8 percent and its share of total international tourism receipts is less than 18 percent. This situation and the fact that the United States continues to have a travel dollar deficit, suggests that the U.S. must strive even harder in the formidable competition for the world travel dollar.

Tourism tends to employ a great number of workers for each dollar of "tourism" that tourists spend. That is, tourism is *labor intensive,* employing considerable labor relative to the other factors of production—capital and land. Tourism employment is concentrated mainly in the service sector rather than the goods-producing sector, and the service sector tends to be less automated. Thus, much labor is used with relatively little capital. In 1976, foreign travelers to the U.S. generated more than 300,000 jobs with payrolls of about $2 billion. Tourism (including both foreign and domestic travelers) is one of the three largest employers in more than thirty states.[5]

The tourism sector is highly diverse, part public, part private, and composed of many industries and many firms. In 1973, the National Tourism Resources Review Commission estimated that there were over 770,000 enterprises involved in tourism, of which 98 percent were classified as small businesses.[6] These small firms include restaurants, hotels and motels, amusement areas, souvenir, gift, and other retail establishments. Thus, unlike the large monopolistic or oligopolistic industries, this sector of the economy closely approximates pure competition.

The tourism sector is *fragmented* as well as competitive; it is an impressive conglomerate of industries represented by many diverse kinds of firms producing many different products. For example, the tourism sector includes transportation, lodging, food, recreation, gifts, and souvenirs. Consequently, there is not always timely or deliberate coordination between the separate firms and industries which make up the tourism sector.[7] Nor is there always systematic coordination between private sector tourism interests and public sector agencies with tourism-related mandates—even though the public sector is the largest operator of tourism facilities such as state and federal parks, forests, seashores, public buildings, monuments, roads, and public transportation. And yet the government sector, consciously or unconsciously, is in the middle of tourism policy decision-making as the political process must resolve numerous issues of concern to the entire society which either affect or are affected by tourism, e.g., environmental protection, energy conservation, and job creation.

Within the United States, individuals frequently purchase tourism goods and services separately. In Europe and in Japan, however, many travelers are using preassembled combinations of services called "packages." Many foreign tourists, especially Japanese, prefer to use inclusive packages when traveling abroad. Demand for packages has spawned the tour operator industry, a segment of the business which assembles and merchandises various combinations of services required by the traveler at, and sometimes enroute to and from, his destination.

The component industries which make up the tourism sector are generally perceived as separate and independent industries. Consequently, there is no Standard Industrial Classification (SIC) code for tourism per se, nor is there universal agreement on which classifications or subclassifications should be included if such a code were to be constructed. As a result, the national income and product accounts data are not compiled on the tourism sector as a whole.

More and more, however, various companies within the tourism sector in the U.S. are merging or acquiring related businesses, thus creating "mini-tourism conglomerates." Pan American, American Airlines, and Trans World Airlines constitute examples of the latter, with their movement into hotels, motels, and tour packaging.

The United States must compete for its share of the international tourist market against other countries which have a more coordinated and planned approach to tourism. Other nations tend to place more emphasis and resources in their national tourism offices than the U.S.

government does through its national tourism office, the United States Travel Service. In addition, many foreign governments own or control a national airline which acts as an arm of the nation's tourism policy. Of the sixty foreign carriers providing service to the U.S., forty-six are either wholly government owned or receive substantial government subsidies, such as government share equity capital, dismissal of loan obligations, et cetera. Many nations work more closely with or own more of their national tourism facilities than does the U.S. An example is the German flag carrier, Lufthansa, which is 80 percent owned by the government; the West German government also owns the railroads which, in turn, license Deutsches Reisbuero (DER), the largest producer of inclusive tour charters in Germany. DER works closely with Lufthansa which wholly owns Condor, a charter airline controlling roughly 85 percent of the German charter market. Finally, Air Tours International, a consortium of the largest German travel agencies, is a major inclusive tour operator founded with Lufthansa assistance.

The bulk (almost 90 percent) of the U.S. international tourism business in 1976 came from ten countries: in order of arrivals, they are Canada, Mexico, Japan, United Kingdom, Germany, France, Australia, Venezuela, Italy, and Brazil.

In 1973, the economies of many of these countries suffered the devastating effects of the Organization of Petroleum Exporting Countries (OPEC) petroleum price increase. Tourism to the U.S. was affected; rates of growth as high as 50 percent and more in the case of Japan in the early 1970s have slid to less than 10 percent. Traffic from some countries experienced no growth whatsoever. By 1976 a recovery was underway.

The growth of tourism is part of the overall shift in the U.S. and other highly industrialized nations from rapid growth in goods-producing industries to rapid growth in the service industries. Services today account for roughly 65 percent of all output produced and consumed in the U.S. and for more than 50 percent of output produced and consumed in Western Europe. The tourism sector is a very important component of the service industries of the American economy.

The travel-tourism sector consists mainly of parts of the larger "service sector" of the economy. As a part of the service sector, tourism is part of the largest and—in some sense—the most dynamic part of the U.S. economy. Victor Fuchs has noted:

The United States is now pioneering in a new stage of economic development. During the period following World War II this country became the first nation in which more than half of the employed population is not involved in the production of . . . tangible goods . . .

The transition from an agricultural to an industrial economy, which began in England and has been repeated in most of the Western world, has been characterized as a "revolution." The shift from industrial to service employment, which had advanced furthest in the United States, but is evident in all developed economies, has proceeded more quietly, but it too has implications for society . . . of "revolutionary" proportions.[8]

The U.S. economy is currently suffering from high unemployment; in the future our economy will require many new jobs to absorb new workers into the labor force. Tourism offers an important source of those new jobs. Tourism is a particularly good potential source of jobs because it is both labor intensive and likely to grow rapidly in the future, which means that for each additional dollar expended on the growing tourism sector, more jobs will be created than in most other areas of the economy.

Tourism has the further advantage that much of the employment in the field tends to be in the hard-to-employ, lower-skilled occupations. These are the occupations which have the highest unemployment rates and which are the most resistant to broad fiscal and monetary policy aimed at lower unemployment. Thus, "microeconomic" efforts concentrated on stimulating the growth of the tourist sector are more likely to create jobs for lower-skilled members of the labor force than the "macroeconomic" measures of tax reduction, government expenditure increases, or increasing the rate of growth of the money supply.

While creating jobs, tourism is an important generator of national income as well. Foreign visitors make large expenditures in the U.S.—about $6.8 billion in 1976—on a wide variety of goods and services, and these yield a substantial increase in income in the U.S.[9] But the overall impact on the U.S. economy is greater than simply the actual expenditure because of the tourism "multiplier." An example of the multiplier effect is as follows. Monsieur A stays at the hotel of Mr. B one night and pays him $20. Mr. B uses part of the $20 to pay Mr. C, a hotel worker. Mr. C uses part of his wages to pay Mr. D, the butcher, who then buys bread from Mr. E, the baker, and the money originally spent by Monsieur A keeps moving through the U.S. economy until it generates a good deal more income than the $20 he spent on the hotel room. There are varying estimates of the magnitude of the tourism multiplier and it will vary from country to country and within a country as well. But it is likely to be between 2.0 and 4.0, meaning that a dollar expended on tourism in the U.S. will increase U.S. GNP between $2 and $4.[10]

The jobs and income created by international tourism can be particularly important for state and local economies, some of which are highly dependent on tourism, and others of which offer great potential for future development. Examples of areas of future growth include more remote areas of scenic beauty, such as Indian reservations and historic areas.

International (and domestic) tourism can become an important tool for creating jobs and increasing income in areas of high unemployment. There are many high unemployment areas of the country which could provide more job opportunities by developing tourism facilities and aggressively promoting their use. One such important area is New England, which is an area of historic interest and scenic beauty. One small step taken February 1977 was approval of a $2,500,000 loan by the Economic Development Administration of the U.S. Department of Commerce to help renovate the Biltmore Hotel in Providence, Rhode Island. This loan is a step toward stimulating the long-term growth of the city through tourism. The loan, however, is just the beginning of the process of increasing tourism in Providence. Renovation of the Biltmore Hotel will have to be supplemented with improvement of other tourist facilities, and then Providence must be promoted as a tourist destination.

On a larger scale, Congress has authorized $50 million, with most of the funds to come from the Economic Development Administration, U.S. Department of Commerce, to support the development of the 1980 Winter Olympics site at Lake Placid, New York. Once the infrastructure for such a development is in place, tourism promotion of the area becomes essential. This is true both prior to and after the Olympics have taken place.

International tourism has a direct and substantial impact on the U.S. balance of payments. The U.S. has historically run a balance of travel deficit, but this deficit has been declining in recent years. In 1976, the travel deficit was still a substantial $2.65 billion, but it was down 15 percent from 1975.[11] The deficit is likely to disappear in the next twenty-five years, mostly because of the attractiveness of the U.S. and the growing real income of people outside the United States. The U.S. economy is in great need of this balance of payments assistance from tourism. In January 1977 the U.S. had the worst month ever in its merchandise balance with a $1.67 billion deficit. This monthly record follows a record annual deficit of $5.87 billion in 1976. Commerce Department economists are predicting an even larger deficit in 1977.[12]

FOREIGN POLICY AND SOCIAL ASPECTS OF INTERNATIONAL TOURISM

Tourism can be an instrument of foreign policy as well as a commercial activity. The French economist, Jean-Maurice Thurot, observed that "tourism is a simple continuation of politics by other means."[13] That is an apt assessment.

Increased contacts between persons of different cultures can lead to increased knowledge and understanding which, in turn, can contribute to a relaxation of tensions between nations. For example, the first step President Carter has taken in reestablishing international relations between the U.S. and Cuba is permitting Americans to travel to Cuba as well as to three Asian countries, Vietnam, North Korea, and Cambodia.[14]

Another recent example is the Shanghai Communique, signed in 1972 by the U.S. and the People's Republic of China. The communique noted, in part: "The effort to reduce tensions is served by improving communication between countries that have different ideologies so as to lessen the risks of confrontation through accident, miscalculation or misunderstanding."[15]

To admit foreign visitors and to facilitate their travel within a nation's borders is a *political* action. It is also an action which, to some extent, is bound to have an impact on domestic politics.

In international politics, fear stems from uncertainty and lack of knowledge. Africa was the mysterious "Dark Continent" to Europeans until Europe sent explorers across the continent and, in the process, found that most of the prior myths disappeared with travel. Similarly, in recent years the travel by Americans to China, even though somewhat limited, has reduced some of the fear and uncertainty about the intentions of the Chinese. This was also part of the intent of the Protocol signed on September 24, 1974, by the U.S. Assistant Secretary of Commerce for Tourism and the Soviet Chairman of the State Administration for Foreign Tourism to the Council of Ministers of the USSR, which called for "the further development of Soviet-American tourism . . . as an expression of the spirit of détente and a constructive force for better mutual understanding and collaboration between the two countries." The Protocol commits both sides "to continue to promote, through all media, the development of two-way travel with higher traffic targets and, also, the creation of adequate conditions for maximum familiarization with the national ways of life and achievements of both countries.[16]

International travel tends to have a moderating effect on the internal policies of foreign governments. An authoritarian regime knows it is being watched and judged by foreign tourists. At the same time a country must be made safe for tourism. Civil strife and disorders, such as those that have wracked Northern Ireland, have a detrimental impact on tourism to such areas.

Tourists create an economic dependence by the host country on tourist-generating countries. This dependence can influence the foreign policy of the host country toward the generating country. This is especially true in nations needing foreign exchange, or hard currency, for economic development. Nations in the process of economic development need to buy key items, especially capital equipment and technology, from the industrial nations in order to speed their own growth. International tourism can be an engine of economic growth by providing an important source of foreign exchange. Most Communist and less-developed nations need tourist dollars for economic growth. Most have currencies which are without value outside of their own nations or currency blocs because they are not freely convertible. Government policy changes can accommodate tourism and thus decrease the need for merchandise exports. For example, the USSR is currently building hotels, training workers to run them, and preparing to provide many other services for the 1980 Summer Olympics. The Olympics are a matter of prestige for the USSR, but they will also be an important source of foreign exchange. After the Olympics the Soviets are likely to promote tourism more aggressively than in the past in order to maintain occupancy rates of Western-style hotels, load factors for Aeroflot planes, and employment levels in tourism-related service jobs.

Tourism has become imbedded in treaties and trade agreements. The most well-known international tourism agreement provisions are contained in the human rights section of the 1975 Helsinki Accord, which was the Final Act of the Conference on Security and Cooperation in Europe. The better-known section of these provisions deals with rights of people to migrate freely, but in the tourism section the thirty-five nations—including the U.S. and the USSR—acknowledged that freer tourism is essential to the development of cooperation between nations. Specifically with reference to tourism, the signatories to the Accord, among other things, (a) expressed their intention to "encourage increased tourism on both an indivdual and group basis," (b) recognized the desirability of carrying out "detailed studies on tourism," (c) agreed to "endeavor, where possible, to ensure that the development of tourism does not injure the artistic, historic and cultural heritage in their respective countries," (d) stated their intention "to facilitate wider travel by their citizens for personal or professional reasons," (e) agreed to "endeavor gradually to lower, where necessary the fees for visas and official travel documents," (f) agreed to "increase, on the basis of appropriate agreements, or arrangements, cooperation in the development of tourism, in particular, by considering bilaterally, possible ways to increase information relating to travel to other countries and to the reception and service of tourists, and other related questions of mutual interest," and (g) expressed their intention "to promote visits to their respective countries."[17]

But the hopes of this Conference and the potential of tourism as an agent of political rapprochement will not come about automatically. They will be realized only through the efforts of governments, national tourist offices, and private industry.

Developing tourism between the U.S. and Communist and less-developed nations, is particularly difficult because these nations have lower per capita income, acute shortages of foreign exchange, and stringent requirements for exit visas. In addition, the U.S. imposes entry restrictions on individuals who are or who have been members of the Communist party. These restrictions were criticized by President Carter in February 1977 as injurious to human rights.

Tourism between the U.S. and these nations will generally not be commercially attractive for years to come. Yet, for political reasons, it is in the U.S. national interest to maintain the highest possible levels of exchange and communication. Governmental efforts have been made to encourage tourism by including tourism provisions in treaties with the USSR, Egypt, and Romania.

Creative efforts at stimulating tourism with Communist and less-developed countries can be made by private industry. An example is a proposed U.S.-USSR tourism agreement sponsored by the U.S. members of the U.S.-USSR Trade and Economic Council at a meeting in Moscow on November 30, 1976. The proposal involves a government-to-government bilateral agreement on tourism development. The centerpiece of the proposal is a "People to People" tourist exchange. Such an exchange would be dependent on institutions and organizations in both countries providing free land arrangements, such as room and board and other accommodations which exclude the need for large amounts of hard currency exchanges. The agreement is an innovative approach to eliminate one stumbling block to Soviet pleasure travel to the U.S.—inadequate hard currency.

A precondition for substantial tourism between any two nations is diplomatic action to smooth the way for tourism as well as for other commercial activities. First, there must be diplomatic recognition of one another by the nations and the establishment of embassies and consulates. The issuance of passports and visas and the ability to travel to other nations is usually controlled by foreign ministries, and, in effect, is a part of a nation's foreign policy. Government can encourage, discourage, or prohibit travel to another nation.

Second, governments must sanction and facilitate a certain level of commercial activity between nations before tourism can proceed. Transportation requires that aviation agreements must be negotiated to facilitate travel. Once a traveler reaches another nation, he must be able to purchase the services he needs. He is in need of banking facilities to exchange money, honor checks, and extend credit.

Governments can eliminate a wide range of currently existing governmental impediments to travel through unilateral action or bilateral or multilateral negotiations. These impediments include: (1)

exit taxes, (2) excessive passport charges, (3) foreign exchange restrictions, (4) visa requirements, and (5) exit and entry restrictions and regulations. Unfortunately, the multilateral international machinery for eliminating barriers to trade in merchandise does not currently address barriers to international commerce in services. Furthermore, U.S. policy analysts have sometimes regarded international tourism as a "nontraded" service because it is "consumed" within the borders of the nation where it is produced. Legal and financial impediments to international travel must be reduced especially if travel between the East and the West is to expand.

Although tourism as a foreign policy tool has a long road ahead, substantial progress has been made on a number of international fronts. A few brief examples will suffice to illustrate this progress. In addition to the agreements already cited, such organizations as the Organization for Economic Cooperation and Development (OECD) and the Organization of American States (OAS) have regular tourism committee meetings.[18] While the OECD tourism policy tends to concentrate more heavily on the economic aspects of tourism, other matters are also dealt with by the Tourism Committee. The OAS conception of tourism is broad as indicated by excerpts from the Extraordinary Session of the Inter-American Travel Congress held in Rio de Janeiro, Brazil, on August 25, 1972, where it was stated that:

> . . . tourism is a cultural, economic, and social force, whose impact on all sectors of society is universally recognized, since it brings into contact peoples of dissimilar backgrounds and standards of living, strengthening relationships, dispelling prejudice, and eschewing arrogance; and that the tourist is an ambassador of the culture of his country, who at the same time, assimilates the culture with which he comes into contact; . . . tourism, in supporting efforts to achieve hemispheric integration and the pursuit of economic goals, complements the high aims of peace and cooperation among the American nations . . . "[19]

On January 2, 1975, an intergovernmental body called the World Tourism Organization (WTO) was established; currently there are ninety-four member nations. WTO is the only organization whose activities cover all sectors of tourism on a worldwide basis. It provides an international forum where tourism officials, whether governmental or not, can discuss problems and exchange ideas. Representatives of the private sector also have access to its membership. Article 3 of the Statutes of WTO states: "The fundamental aim of the Organization shall be the promotion and development of tourism with a view to contributing to economic development, international understanding, peace, prosperity, and universal respect for, and observance of, human rights and fundamental freedoms for all without distinction as to race, sex, language or religion. The Organization shall take all appropriate action to attain this objective."[20]

There has been increasing interest in recent years in the impact of tourism on the environment. More discussion has dwelled on environmental degradation caused by tourism than on positive aspects of tourism. The report of the 1973 European Travel Commission Conference on Tourism and Conservation stated articulately both the positive and negative factors in the interdependent relationship between tourism and the environment:

> First, . . . environment is the indispensable basis, the major attraction for tourism. Without an attractive environment, there would be no tourism. . . .
>
> Second, . . . the interests of tourism demand the protection of the scenic and historic heritage. The offer in the travel brochure must be genuine. . . .
>
> In some countries, tourism . . . is seen by those concerned to protect the environment as their powerful ally. The desire to gain national income from tourism can impel governments to protect monuments or natural areas they might otherwise have neglected.
>
> Third, tourism can directly assist active conservation . . . can prompt men to contribute towards . . . conservation . . . of [famous places such as] Florence and . . . Venice. The entry fees of tourists help to maintain historic structures and parks. . . . Tourist activity may provide new uses for old buildings. . . .
>
> And yet, despite these positive links, many conservationists feel that tourism can present a major threat to the environment . . . that countless hotels, roads and other facilities provided for the tourists ruin the beauties of the seacoast, disturb the peace of the country, and rob the mountains of their serene grandeur . . . streets choked with tourist traffic, and . . . squares and marketplaces turned into parks for visitors.[21]

The challenge for tourism in the next twenty-five years is to plan and develop it and to invest in tourism facilities to improve rather than degrade the environment.

PROJECTIONS AND IMPLICATIONS OF INTERNATIONAL TOURISM THROUGH 2000

Projections

Making long-run projections is a very uncertain business. Tomorrow is unknown to us, and the more tomorrows we put together, the more likely it is that events will take an unexpected turn. But the prognosticator Herman Kahn has looked at the next twenty-five years of tourism. He predicts that, by the year 2000, "Tourism will be one of the largest industries in the world, if not the largest" and that it should " . . . continue its current trend to increase by 10 to 20 percent a year" until that time.[22]

Rapid growth in international tourism has also been forecast by Anthony Edwards in a recent study.[23] He predicts that globally the growth rate of travel is likely to be considerably faster from 1974 to 1980 than was true from 1966 to 1974. He goes on to suggest that the growth rate for the period 1980 to 1985 will taper off, but still remain a little higher than was true for 1966 to 1974.

Projections of future developments in tourism for the next twenty-five years have been made by staff of the United States Travel Service. These forecasts were made assuming relatively "steady state" growth in the economies of the U.S. and of those nations of the world which are the major sources of tourist visitors to the U.S. Within the U.S., the basic economic assumptions are of moderate rates of increase both in the real income growth of the economy and in the price level. Growth in real GNP is assumed to remain at approximately the average post-World War II rate. Inflation is expected to be well below the high rates of the mid-1970s. It is also assumed that there will be no major natural disasters or other catastrophic effects on the tourism industry, including another major energy crisis, and that international impediments to travel will not increase.

Foreign visitor arrivals to the U.S. and foreign tourism receipts will increase substantially over the next twenty-five years. Arrivals were 17.5 million in 1976; in the year 2000 they are estimated to more than double to 43.0 million. Foreign tourism receipts were $6.8 billion in 1976. In the year 2000, this figure would nearly triple to $19.5 billion in 1976 dollars.

Table 7.1   Foreign Visitor Arrivals to the U.S., 1950-2000

YEAR	ARRIVALS	5-YEAR AVERAGE ANNUAL GROWTH
1950	2,736,000	—
1955	5,431,000	15.3%
1960	6,503,072	3.7
1965	7,841,565	4.2
1970	12,362,299	9.6
1975	15,698,118	4.9
1976	17,523,239	—
1977	18,600,000(e)	—
1980	22,030,000(e)	7.8(e)
1985	27,270,000(e)	4.4(e)
1990	32,510,000(e)	3.6(e)
1995	37,755,000(e)	3.0(e)
2000	43,000,000(e)	2.6(e)

SOURCE: Research and Analysis Division, United States Travel Service, U.S. Department of Commerce

The forecasted growth in foreign visitor arrivals to the U.S. as shown in Table 7.1 and Fig. 7.1, are based on a number of key variables including: worldwide population, past tourism trends, anticipated business cycle movements and economic trends, country-by-country expected travel patterns and characteristics, and the growth in air transportation package and charter traffic to the U.S.

Forecasts of foreign tourism receipts, as illustrated in Table 7.2 and Fig. 7.2, were made using a disaggregated approach, estimating Canadian, Mexican, and overseas expenditures separately and then summing the three separate estimates; estimates were made including transportation in current dollars. Receipt estimates were first made on

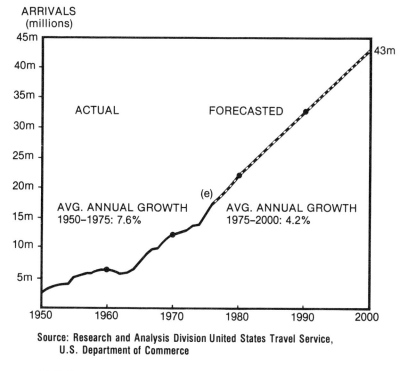

Fig. 7.1 Total Foreign Visitors to the U.S.: 1950-2000

a *per capita* basis in each of the three markets separately, and these per capita estimates were then multiplied by the foreign visitor arrivals to yield *total* receipts.

Among the key assumptions regarding tourism receipts were: (1) that the real growth in U.S. tourism receipts will be more rapid than arrivals due to increasing real disposable income, and (2) that transportation receipts will grow at approximately the same rate as foreign arrivals.

For both arrivals and receipts, it is assumed that the rate of growth during the period 1975-2000 is gradually declining. The average annual rate of growth for the entire period is 4.2 percent for foreign visitor arrivals and 4.5 percent in real terms for foreign tourism receipts. In both cases this represents a substantial decline in the rate of growth

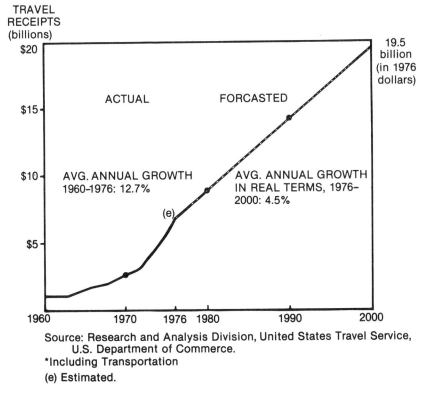

Source: Research and Analysis Division, United States Travel Service,
U.S. Department of Commerce.
*Including Transportation
(e) Estimated.

Fig. 7.2 Foreign Tourism Receipts: 1960-2000*

from previous periods, arrivals having grown at an average annual
rate of 7.6 percent between 1950 and 1976, and foreign tourism receipts having grown by 12.7 percent in current dollars and 8.2 percent
in real dollars between 1960 and 1976. It should be noted that these
projections are considerably more conservative than those of Herman
Kahn and Anthony Edwards. Even such conservative estimates show
substantial growth in international tourism over the next twenty-five
years. As is clearly shown by these estimates, international tourism will
continue to be a dynamic sector of the U.S. economy. International
tourism will be growing more rapidly than the U.S. economy as a
whole, and tourism will become increasingly important in the international sector of the U.S. economy.

Table 7.2   Foreign Tourism Receipts: 1960-2000

YEAR	TRAVEL RECEIPTS (Including Transportation) (Millions)	5-YEAR AVERAGE ANNUAL GROWTH Current Dollars	Constant (Real) Dollars
1960	$ 1,025	—	—
1965	1,545	8.8%	—
1970	2,708	12.0	—
1975	5,606	16.0	—
1976	6,743	—	—
1980(e)	8,915(e)	—	9.6(e)
1985(e)	11,560(e)	—	5.3(e)
1990(e)	14,210(e)	—	4.2(e)
1995(e)	16,850(e)	—	3.5(e)
2000(e)	19,500(e)	—	3.0(e)

SOURCE: Research and Analysis Division, United States Travel Service, U.S. Department of Commerce

(e)   Estimated.

Implications of Projections

There are wide implications which stem from the expected developments in tourism in the next twenty-five years. Among the more important are the following:

First, international tourism may be reaching the point which in terms of economic development, Walt Rostow called the "takeoff" into sustained growth, such that by the year 2000 we may reach a period of mass consumption of tourism.[24] This trend should be strongly supported by the anticipated relative decrease in the cost of transportation and the large increases in real per capita income.

In the year 2000 the real income per person throughout the world will be much higher than it is today. As a result there will be a much larger amount of discretionary income available for activities such as pleasure travel. This discretionary income will be spread more widely across the income distribution than it is today; this will result in a larger proportion of the world's population traveling than travels today. International tourists will include more individuals from the lower end of the income distribution as well as those from the upper end who form the bulk of today's travelers.

Assuming that aircraft technology and price reduction policies outstrip increases in the cost of jet fuel, the relative cost of tourism will be declining over the next twenty-five years, particularly in the area of transportation. A decline in the price of tourism is important because the growth sector of air travel is in pleasure travel, which is sensitive to price as well as insensitive to time. Price is of paramount importance, and scheduling is less important because pleasure travel plans generally are made with considerable advance planning.[25]

New and cheaper forms of transportation are already beginning to appear. The Advanced Booking Charters (ABCs) are already sharply reducing the price of international tourism and promise to develop a much larger market than existed just a few months ago.[26]

In the future, international tourism is likely to be much more commonplace and casual than it is today. As a result, cheaper and more informal methods of transportation are likely to appear; an example is Freddie Laker's "Skytrain" concept which is a very cheap, one-way, no-frills trans-Atlantic shuttle, little different than the current shuttle service between Los Angeles and San Francisco or New York and Washington, D.C.[27]

A system like Skytrain—with a London-New York fare of around $135—could bring far more visitors to the U.S. For example, Skytrain could bring Europeans to the U.S. for a weekend for single-stop tourism, such as to attend plays in New York City, Mardi Gras in New Orleans, the Indianapolis 500, or the Kentucky Derby.

Second, as a result of much more widespread international tourism, there will be greater international personal contact and knowledge about the rest of the world. There will be greater cosmopolitanism and less provincialism in the sense that traveling widely will be the expectation of great numbers of people, and little of the world will be totally unknown or unfamiliar. There will be no "Dark Continents" because travel will shed light on the darkness. There will be a much greater possibility for creating a world of international understanding.

Third, the economic impact of international tourism will be greater than it is today. International tourism will become a more important part of the world economy as tourism grows more rapidly than real per capita income. There will be several results: First, a larger portion of jobs and income will derive directly from international tourism. Second, the impact on the balance of payments will be greater. For the U.S. this would mean that a growing proportion of our export earnings would come from selling tourism services—to foreign tourists in the U.S.—rather than from exporting merchandise. And selected state and local economies would be heavily supported by international tourism.

Fourth, the role of international politics will have a great impact on the international tourism sector. Tourism may become even more sensitive to the policies of governments as it grows in size. Impediments to travel such as control of visas, passports, and foreign exchange will have the ability to stymie travel. Alternatively, elimination or amelioration of these impediments will have the power to facilitate tourism. More nations are likely to have bilateral trade negotiations which include agreements to mutually reduce the impediments to travel.

Fifth, environmental issues will become increasingly important. As the number of tourists increase, the problem of "crowding" in tourist areas could become acute, especially in areas which are limited spatially or in ability to absorb large numbers of people. Fragile natural environments such as the Alaskan frozen tundra or the Rocky Mountain soil above the timberline can be trampled and destroyed by tourist hordes. Museums and public buildings can quickly become overcrowded. There will be a greater need to plan for tourist growth to ease crowding and prevent damage to the natural environment. One step in this direction is to reduce the seasonality of tourism.[28]

Sixth, a related problem is the *absorptive capacity* of an economy with respect to tourism. This questions the ability of an area to supply enough tourist infrastructure and facilities to handle the demand of tourists. There can be limitations because of labor shortages, capital shortages, land shortages, et cetera. These shortages can be due to natural scarcity. There may also be alternative uses of resources which the local population finds preferable to setting them aside for tourism. Such resistance to using resources to increase absorptive capacity relative to tourism could become particularly important if local opposition to tourism increases because of environmental concerns.

CONCLUSIONS AND RECOMMENDATIONS

The future of international tourism is bright. Tourism has been growing rapidly in the post-World War II period, and it should continue its dynamic growth through the year 2000. While there is inadequate public knowledge about the economic and social importance of tourism, that industry has recently been getting more attention from the public and from governmental bodies recognizing its existing and growing stature.

For example, the United States Travel Service was only established in 1961. Prior to that date there was no coordinated U.S. national tourism policy regarding international tourism. Compared to other nations, the U.S. has been a latecomer to tourism public policy.

The U.S. is now starting to catch up: on July 9, 1975, the United States Travel Service was authorized to conduct a domestic tourism program. This program, designed to encourage Americans to travel within their own country, complements the agency's fifteen-year-old thrust of promoting international travel to the U.S. In effect, the U.S. Department of Commerce through the United States Travel Service can now deal with all aspects of tourism to and within the U.S.

The U.S. government has also been giving increasing attention to thinking and rethinking its national tourism objectives and strategies. From 1971 to 1973, the National Tourism Resources Review Commission conducted a major study of tourism needs and the resources to meet those needs. The commission published a major study, a six-volume report of its findings.[29] Currently, the U.S. Senate is conducting a major study of federal government policy toward tourism, the National Tourism Policy Study. This study was authorized by the Senate in June 1974, and it is scheduled to be completed in 1977 or early 1978. Its aim is to develop a national tourism policy which "should be a prescription for assuring that the Federal tourism effort effectively responds to the national interests in tourism and, where appropriate, meets the needs of State and local governments and the private sector of industry."[30] At the same time, as was mentioned earlier in this paper, there has been increasing worldwide appreciation of the importance of tourism. This increased recognition has included the conversion of the International Union of Official Travel Organizations into the World Tourism Organization (WTO) in 1975. WTO is a full-fledged intergovernmental body constituted to look at tourism issues from a worldwide perspective. WTO was designed to provide a framework for governmental consultations, effective cooperation between member states, and formulation of decisions on questions relating to their policies in the sphere of tourism.[31] There are also regional multilateral bodies on tourism, such as the Organization of American States, Organization for Economic Cooperation and Development, and other organizations, which recognize that tourism is an instrument of economic and social development.

New directions in tourism have not just come from governmental and international program-policy bodies, but also from tourism research which is the basis for developing new policies and programs. This research has substantiated the economic, political, and social importance of tourism. On the economic front, one recent study noted "the recent trend to emphasize the role of service sectors in development planning, and in particular the recent emphasis on the development of tourism as a desirable strategy."[32]

This strategy includes both the building of tourist facilities and the promotion of tourism. As nations concentrate increased resources on economic development through the encouragement of tourism, the tourism sector should receive an additional impetus for future growth.

All of these developments will help to bring about—indeed, will force—a greater degree of tourism planning within the United States. Similarly, it is probable that those states with tourism-based economies will, like Hawaii, develop plans for assuring the quality of life for both tourists and their host communities. Tourism is simply too important an industry to permit it to develop without planning and policy direction.

In the past, the U.S. national interest with respect to tourism has received low priority; segments of the far-flung U.S. international tourism industry have operated at a competitive disadvantage in the international marketplace; and the full potential of tourism as a U.S. diplomatic tool and force for détente remains largely unrealized.

What changes, if any, should the United States be prepared to make with respect to tourism policy planning? There is no single recommendation that would signal a particular path that should be followed. However, with the potential that tourism offers in international economic and foreign policy, it is clear that the role of government must be one of acting as a catalytic agent that will: (1) coordinate the tourism industry which, while fragmented, must compete in the international marketplace with government-supported programs of other countries; (2) respond positively to the winds of change that buffet worldwide tourism; and (3) lead the quest for international cooperative arrangements that will foster greater flows of tourists. And because of the dynamic economic and political developments taking place, it is imperative that the U.S. adopt a strong, positive stance on tourism and that it vigorously pursue its legitimate tourism interests.

There are only two basic options with respect to international tourism policy: (a) maintain a stance of laissez-faire toward the U.S. international travel industry; or (b) use diplomatic and other governmental channels to advance the cause of U.S. tourism interests and create an environment in which U.S.-owned firms can compete more effectively for the world's international tourism business. Obviously, our course should be the second option.

Specifically, the United States should: (1) pursue the elimination or the reduction of impediments to the sale of international tourism services, such as currency and customs allowances, negotiation of a General Agreement on Tariffs and Trade (GATT) type of agreement on tourism, or via trade talks conducted under GATT aegis; (2) seek reciprocal reduction of barriers to East-West tourism, such as exit permits, admission restrictions, certain visa requirements, and off limit policies restricting free movement; and (3) maintain a flexible posture on tourism issues as regards the Third World where, in some cases, commercial and political interests are on a collision course.

NOTES

1. On January 10, 1977, during hearings before the Committee on Commerce, United States Senate, 95th Congress, First Session, the Secretary of Commerce stated:

While tourism is primarily a commercial activity, it has a broad range of economic, political, and social implications—both on the domestic and on the international fronts. The role of government should be that of a catalytic agent that will coordinate the tourism industry which, while fragmented, must compete in the international marketplace with government-supported programs of other countries.

2. A technical discussion of quantitive approaches to policy and planning in the tourism sector is contained in the following publications: (1) an article on "Public Policy Planning and Operations Research in the Tourism Sector: Never the Twain Shall Meet—Or Shall They?" presented at the 1976 joint ORSA/TIMS Conference, Miami Beach, Florida, November 3-6, by David L. Edgell, Charles E. Gearing, Rodney Stiefbold, and William W. Swart and published by the Department of Management Science, School of Business Administration, University of Miami, Coral Gables, Florida; and (2) Charles E. Gearing, William W. Swart, and Turgut Var's book, *Planning for Tourism Development: Quantitive Approaches* (New York: Praeger Publishers, 1976).

3. In this paper the term *tourism* is used synonymously with all aspects of travel and tourism unless otherwise specified.

4. Tourism as a basic activity to the quality of life has been duly recognized in planning for the 1980 World Conference on Tourism, the agenda of which includes the following items:

. . . clarify the implications of tourism for the national and international society of the present day, with regard to the individual, human relations, education, culture and politics, and identify tourism's role in individual and group relations within countries and also between nations; bring out the responsibilities incumbent on governments, extending beyond the purely economic and commerical aspects of tourism. . . .

5. Douglas C. Frechtling, "Travel as an Employer in the State Economy," mimeographed (Washington, D.C.: U.S. Travel Data Center, 1976).

6. National Tourism Resources Review Commission, *Destination USA* (Washington, D.C.: U.S. Government Printing Office).

7. For a discussion of the lack of tourism planning, see Clare A. Gunn, "Industry Fragmentation vs. Tourism Planning," mimeographed (College Station, Tex.: Texas A & M, 1976).

8. Victor Fuchs, *The Service Economy* (New York: National Bureau of Economic Research, 1968), pp. 1-2.

9. U.S. Travel Service, Department of Commerce, preliminary figure.

10. Estimates of the size of the tourism multiplier can be found in Robert W. McIntosh, *Tourism Principles, Practices and Philosophies.* (Columbus, Ohio: Grid, 1973), pp. 184-87. Estimates for given nations and states tend to run between 1.5 and 3.5, but go to a high of 4.3.

11. U.S. Travel Service, Department of Commerce.

12. *Wall Street Journal,* 1 March 1977, p. 2.

13. *Economia,* May 1975.

14. *Washington Post,* 9 March 1977, p. 1.

15. Shanghai Communique (February 27, 1972), joint statement issued at the conclusion of President Richard M. Nixon's visit to China.

16. This memorandum of understanding was signed on September 24, 1974, by the U.S. Assistant Secretary of Commerce for Tourism, C. Langhorne Washburn, and the Soviet Chairman of the State Administration for Foreign Tourism to the Council of Ministers of the USSR, Sergei S. Nikitin.

17. The *Conference on Security and Cooperation in Europe Final Act* (commonly referred to as the "Helsinki Accord") was signed by 35 nations, including the U.S., on August 1, 1975, in Helsinki.

18. The OECD and OAS are essentially regional international bodies. The OAS is a truly regional organization, its members all being from the Western Hemisphere; as such it focuses its attention on tourism to and within the Americas. The OECD, on the other hand, originated as a European regional international organization but now includes the United States, Canada, and Japan as well as most Western European nations. This membership means that the organization represents the major western industrial nations. The scope of the OECD tourism policy reflects the interests of the people of the western industrial nations who do the vast majority of international traveling.

19. The Declaration of "Rio de Janeiro" resulted from the Inter-American Travel Congress (OAS) meeting in Rio de Janeiro, Brazil, on August 25, 1972.

20. World Tourism Organization, *Statutes,* Article 3, p. 2, September 27, 1970, Mexico City.

21. European Travel Commission, *Tourism and Conservation: Working Together,* London, 1974.

22. Herman Kahn, William Brown, Leon Martel, *The Next 200 Years: A Scenario for America and the World* (New York: William Morrow and Company, 1976), p. 40.

23. Anthony Edwards, *International Tourism Development: Forecasts to 1985.* (London: Economic Intelligence Unit, Special Report, 1976).

24. Walt W. Rostow, *The Stages of Economic Growth.* (Cambridge and New York: Cambridge University Press, 1960).

25. "Air Transport and Tourism" in the 1976 *International Economic Report of the President* (Washington, D.C., January 1977), Chapter 10.

26. The ABCs represent the newest form of nonscheduled air transport service. They represent an "advance" in the development of charter service in that they are non-

affinity charters—travelers do not have to belong to organized groups to take advantage of the lower fares. Fare reductions have been appearing on scheduled service as well. Reduced fares have appeared in intrastate service which does not have to be approved by the Civil Aeronautics Board (CAB). Recently the CAB has approved the American Airline "Super Saver" transcontinental fare which will reduce substantially the cost of travel between the East and West coasts.

27. For a fuller discussion of Skytrain, see *Time* magazine, 31 January 1977.

28. Attempts to reduce the seasonality in tourism are underway in Europe. For a discussion of German efforts in this area, see Organization for Economic Cooperation and Development, Tourism Committee, "Staggering Holidays," mimeographed (Paris, January 1977).

29. National Tourism Resources Review Commission, *Destination USA* (Washington, D.C.: U.S. Government Printing Office).

30. U.S. Senate, Committee on Commerce, *A Conceptual Basis for the National Tourism Policy Study* (Washington, D.C.: U.S. Government Printing Office, 1976).

31. World Tourism Organization, Article 3 "Aims" in *Statutes,* Mexico City, 27 September 1977.

32. Moheb A. Ghali, "Tourism and Economic Growth: An Empirical Study," *Economic Development and Cultural Change,* vol. 24, no. 3 (April 1976), pp. 527-38.